Reasoning Olympiad

Highly useful for all school students participating
in Various Olympiads & Competitions

Series Editor Keshav Mohan
Author Amogh Goel

Class
3

arihant
ARIHANT PRAKASHAN, MEERUT

ARIHANT PRAKASHAN, MEERUT

Administrative & Production Offices

Corporate Office 'Ramchhaya' 4577/15, Agarwal Road, Darya Ganj New Delhi -110002
Tele: 011- 47630600, 43518550; Fax: 011- 23280316

Head Office Kalindi, TP Nagar, Meerut (UP) - 250002
Tele: 0121-2401479, 2512970, 4004199; Fax: 0121-2401648

All disputes subject to Meerut (UP) jurisdiction only.

Sales & Support Offices

Agra, Ahmedabad, Bengaluru, Bhubaneswar, Bareilly, Chennai, Delhi, Guwahati, Haldwani, Hyderabad, Jaipur, Jalandhar, Jhansi, Kolkata, Kota, Lucknow, Meerut, Nagpur & Pune

ISBN 978-93-5251-212-6

Price ₹50

Typeset by Arihant DTP Unit at Meerut
Printed & Bound by Arihant Publications (I) Ltd. (Press Unit)

Production Team

Publishing Manager	Mahendra Singh Rawat	*Page Layouting*	Krishna Kumar Saini
Project Head	Mona Yadav	*DTP Operator*	Shravan Pandey & Ravindar Rawat
Project Coordinator	Akanksha Jain	*Cover Designer*	Syed Darin Zaidi
Proof Reader	Sachin Kumar Prajapati, Gara Sharma	*Inner Designer*	Deepak Kumar

For further information about the products from Arihant
log on to www.arihantbooks.com or email to info@arihantbooks.com

Preface

Reasoning Olympiad Series for Class 2nd-10th is a series of books, which will challenge the young inquisitive minds by the non-routine and exciting Reasoning or Logic based problems.

The main purpose of this series is to make the students ready for competitive exams, as Reasoning is an integral section of almost all competitive examinations. All the questions given in this series are objective in nature so, they will provide students a feel of competitive examinations as school/board exams are of qualifying nature, but not competitive, which mainly have Objective Questions.

- **Need of Olympiad Series**
  This series helps students, who are willing to sharpen their problem solving skills through logical thinking. Unlike typical assessment books, which emphasise on drilling practice, the focus of this series is on practising problem solving techniques.

- **Development of Logical Approach**
  The thought provoking questions given in this series will help students to attain a deeper understanding of the concepts and through, which students will be able to imbibe reasoning/Logical/Analytical skills in themselves.

- **Complement Your School Studies**
  This series complements the additional preparation needs of students for regular school/board exams. As most of the schools conduct aptitude test on a regular basis. Along with, it will also address all the requirements of the students, who are approaching National/State level competitions or Olympiads.

I shall welcome criticism from the students, teachers, educators and parents. I would also like to hear from all of you about errors and short comings, which may have remained in this edition and the suggestions for their improvement in the next edition.

Editor

CONTENT

CHAPTER

1

Matching Pairs

'Matching Pairs' as the name suggests means similarity between the elements in the first pair and the elements in the second pair. Students are required to find the similarity and complete the second pair in the same way as the first pair.

Example 1 Identify the relation between the objects in the first pair and then find the object that will replace the question mark.

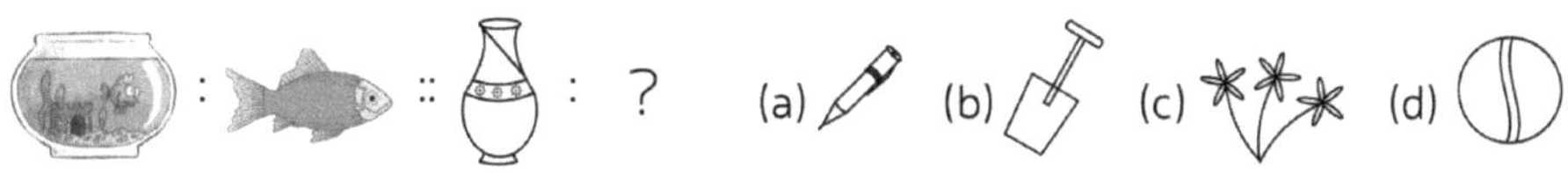

Sol. As fishes are kept in aquarium. Similarly, flowers are kept in flower pot.
Hence, option (c) is correct.

Example 2 Two numbers/letters written in the arrow are related to each other. Find the missing term in the second arrow following the same rule.

(i) 6 : 24 : 9 : ? (a) 36 (b) 27 (c) 45 (d) 35

(ii) D : W : H : ? (a) G (b) U (c) S (d) Z

Sol. (i) As, $6 \times 4 = 24$, similarly $9 \times 4 = 36$. So, the missing number is 36.
Hence, option (a) is correct.

(ii) As, 'D' is fourth letter from the starting in the English alphabet and 'W' is fourth letter from the end. Similarly, 'H' is eighth letter from the starting and 'S' is eighth letter from the end. So, 'S' is the missing letter.
Hence, option (c) is correct.

Note Following table showing letters position in English alphabetical series will help the students to solve these type of questions.

Forward	1	2	3	4	5	6	7	8	9	10	11	12	13	14	15	16	17	18	19	20	21	22	23	24	25	26
Alphabet	A	B	C	D	E	F	G	H	I	J	K	L	M	N	O	P	Q	R	S	T	U	V	W	X	Y	Z
Backward	26	25	24	23	22	21	20	19	18	17	16	15	14	13	12	11	10	9	8	7	6	5	4	3	2	1

Let's Practice

1. Find the picture which will complete the second pair in the same way as the first pair.

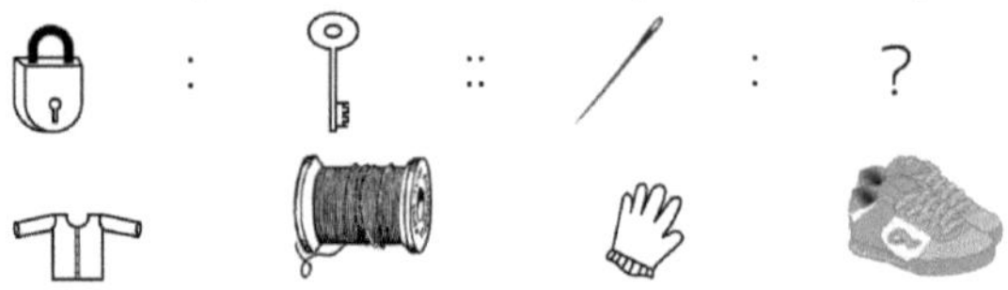

(a) (b) (c) (d)

2. Complete the second pair in the same way as first pair.

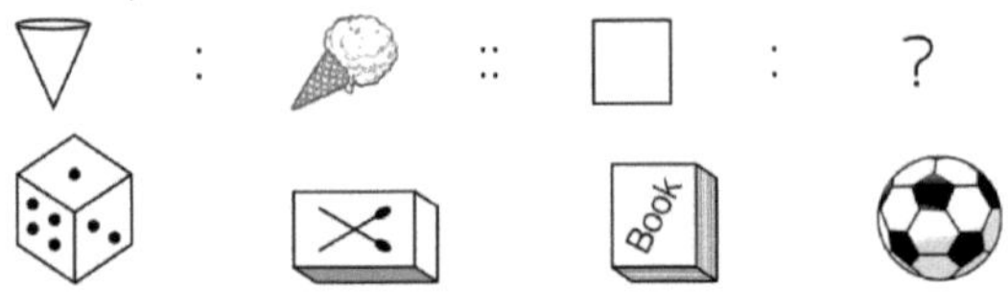

(a) (b) (c) (d)

3. Which pattern from the given options will complete the second pair in the same way as the first pair?

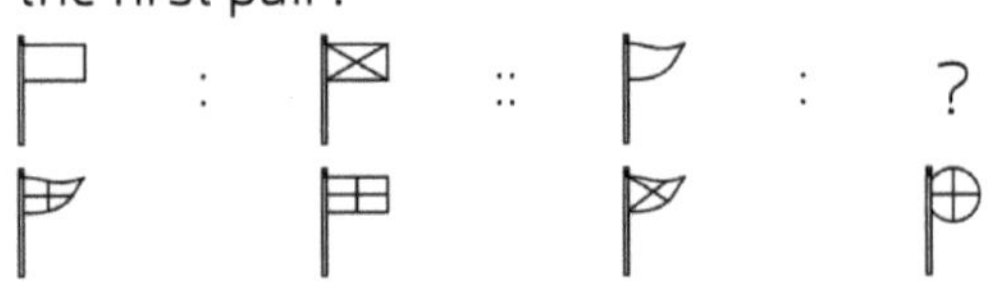

(a) (b) (c) (d)

4. Look at the given figures carefully, then identify the relation between the first two figures and find the missing figure.

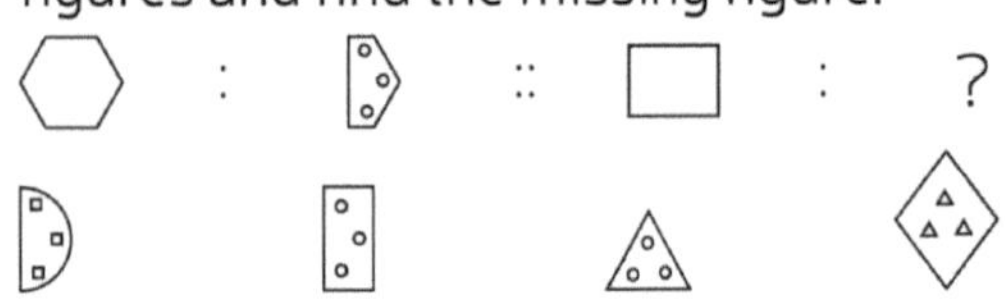

(a) (b) (c) (d)

5. Which pattern will complete the second pair in the same way as the first pair?

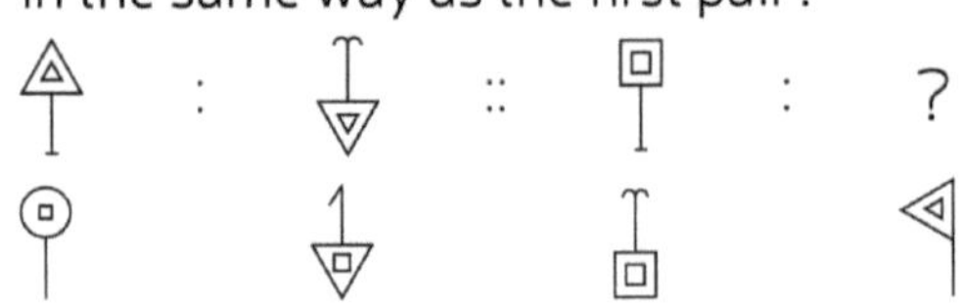

(a) (b) (c) (d)

6. The numbers written on the first and second balloons are related to each other in a certain way. Find the number that should be written in the fourth balloon following the same pattern which first two follow.

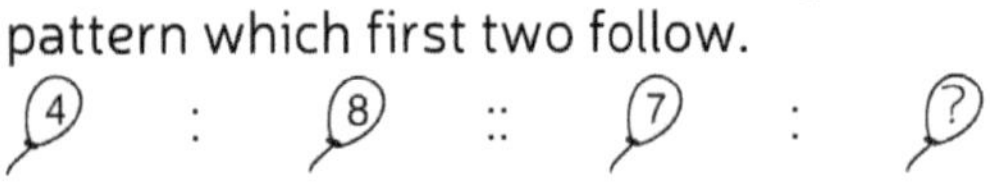

(a) 11 (b) 14 (c) 16 (d) 21

7. Ice-cream prices are shown on the ice-creams. First two are related to each other. Find the price of fourth ice-cream following the pattern which first two follow.

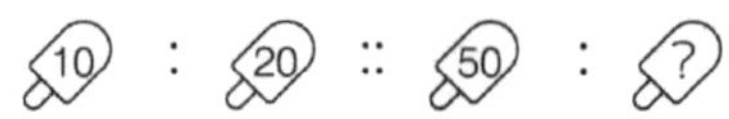

(a) 40 (b) 60 (c) 55 (d) 45

8. Some letters shown below in each box are related to each other. Find the missing letter.

PQ : R :: DE : ?

(a) T (b) M (c) G (d) F

9. Letters given below are linked to each other in the pair. Identify the relation and then find the missing letters.

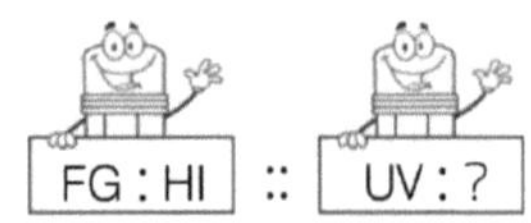

(a) XY (b) VW (c) WX (d) TU

10. What should come in place of question mark such that the second pair follows the same pattern which first pair follows?

C3 : E5 :: I9 : ?

(a) H8 (b) J10 (c) G7 (d) K11

11. Some letters are written on the toffees shown below. Identify the relation between the letters on the first toffee and then find the missing letters.

(a) LMN (b) MNO
(c) JMO (d) GHI

12. TRAIN is to RAIN, as PAGE is to ?.
(a) GEA (b) AGE (c) GAP (d) PAG

13. Onion is to Vegetable, as Cherry is to ?
(a) Tree (b) Fruit (c) Jam (d) Pastry

14. Tongue is to Taste, as Ears is to ?
(a) Sense (b) Feel (c) Look (d) Hear

15. Bird is to Sky, as Duck is to ?
(a) Water (b) Swim
(c) Quack (d) Fly

CHAPTER 2

Odd One Out

'Odd One Out' means finding a term/figure from the given group of figures/terms, which does not belong to the group.

Example 1 From the given alternatives, find which one is different from others.

(a)

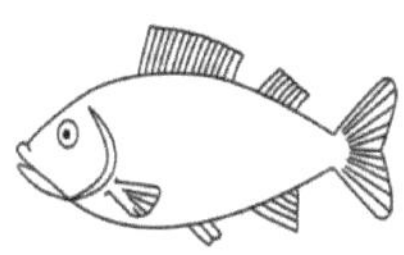

(b)

(c)

(d)

Sol. Beetle, ant and spider are insects and found on land, but fish is an aquatic animal i.e. found under water.

So, it is different from others.

Hence, option (b) is correct.

Example 2 Find which number on the chart is different from others.

(a)

(b)

(c)

(d)

Sol. Except 97, all the numbers have 9 at one's place while in 97, 9 is at ten's place.

Hence, option (b) is correct.

Example 3 Which pair of letters does not belong to the group?

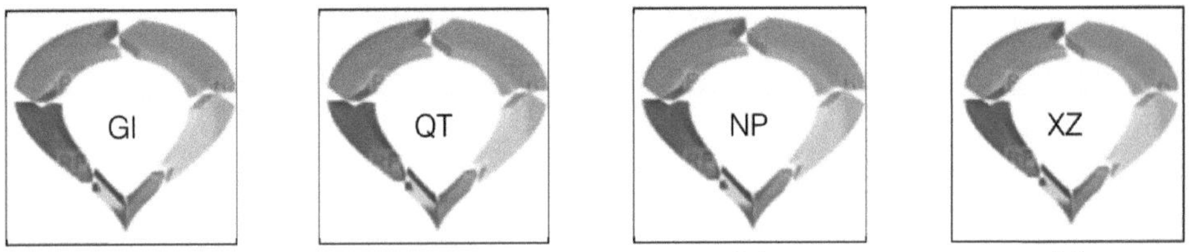

(a) (b) (c) (d)

Sol. The pattern is as follows

$$G \xrightarrow[H]{} I, Q \xrightarrow[R,S]{} T, N \xrightarrow[O]{} P, X \xrightarrow[Y]{} Z$$

Here, letters' pair QT follows different pattern.

So, QT does not belong to the group.

Hence, option (b) is correct.

Example 4 Identify the one that does not belong to the group.

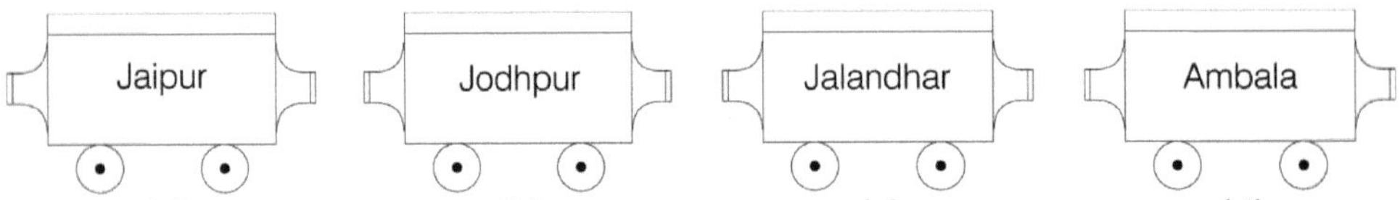

(a) (b) (c) (d)

Sol. The names of Jaipur, Jodhpur and Jalandhar start with letter J while the name of Ambala starts with letter A.

Hence, option (d) is correct.

Example 5 Identify the one that does not belong to the group.

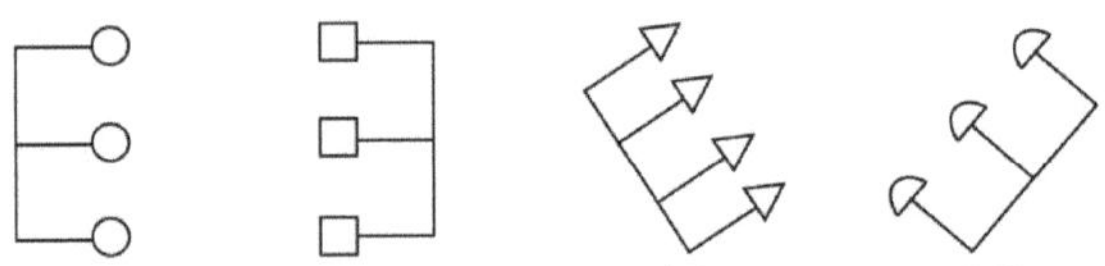

(a) (b) (c) (d)

Sol. In figures (a), (b) and (d), the number of shapes attached with lines is three, while in figure (c) it is four.

So, figure (c) does not belong to the group.

Hence, option (c) is correct.

Let's Practice

1. Following pictures are there on a wall in a classroom. Find a picture, which is different from others.

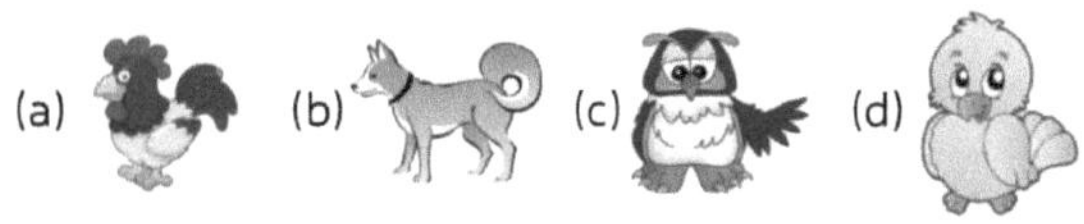

2. Among the clocks shown below three are same in a certain way and one is different. Find that clock, which is different from others.

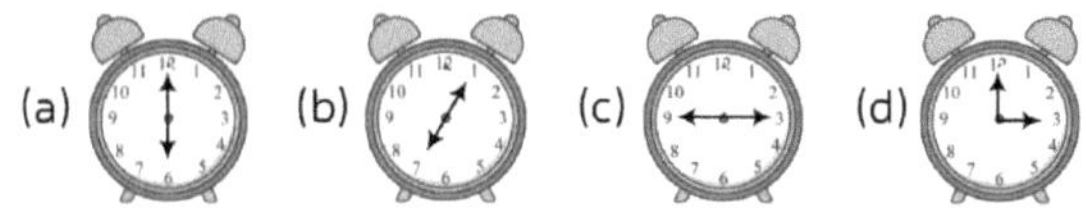

3. Find which pose of sparrow is different from others.

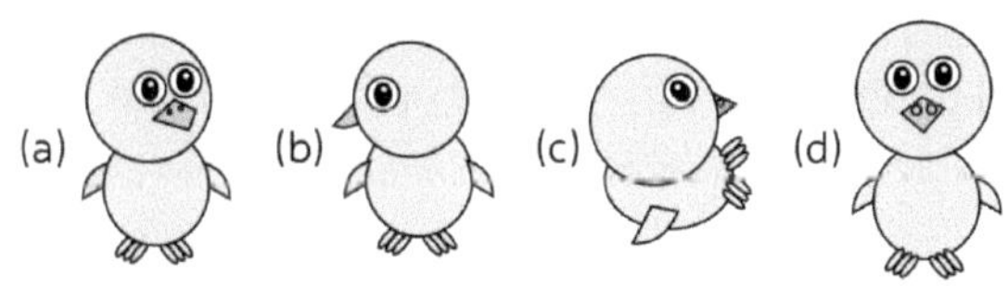

4. In a drawing book, following shapes are given. Find that figure, which is different from others in the group.

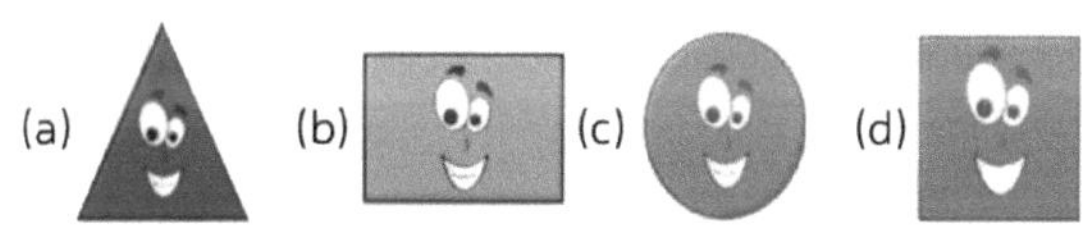

5. A child draws following shapes in its drawing notebook and keep the one side, which is different from others. Find that shape from the given shapes.

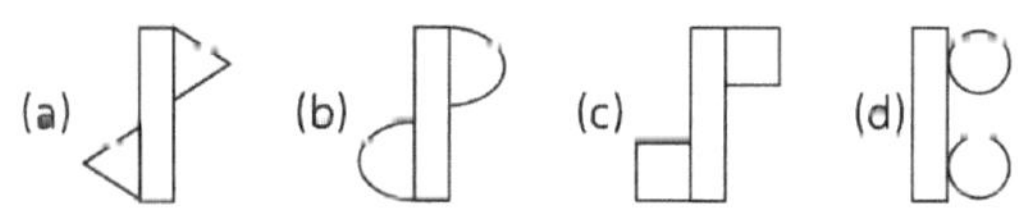

6. Which figure from the given alternatives is different from others in the group?

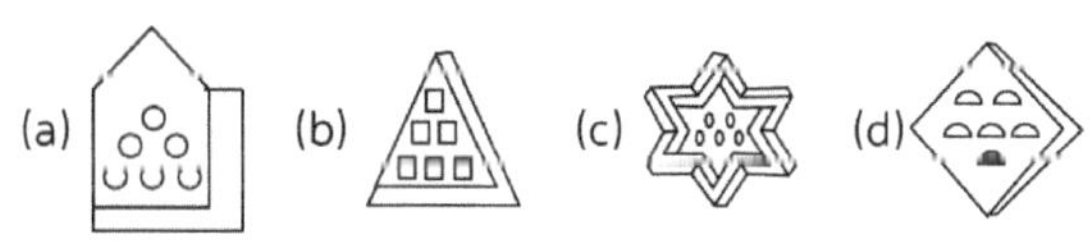

7. Find the letter which is different from others.

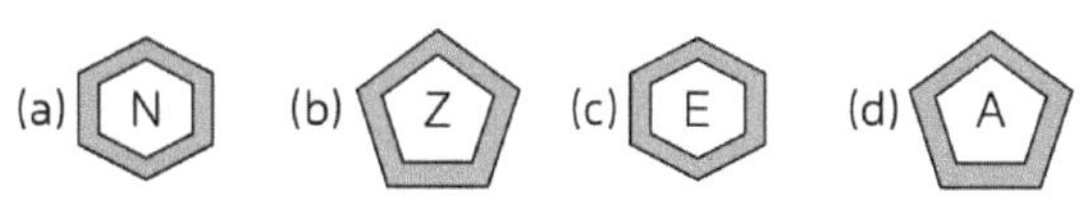

8. Some letters are given in different shapes. Find that group of letters which is different.

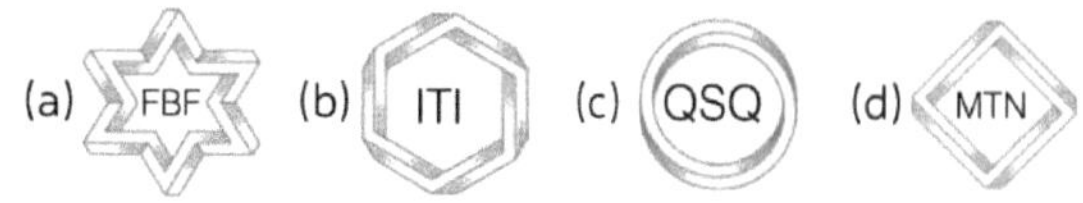

9. Which one is different from the given alternatives?

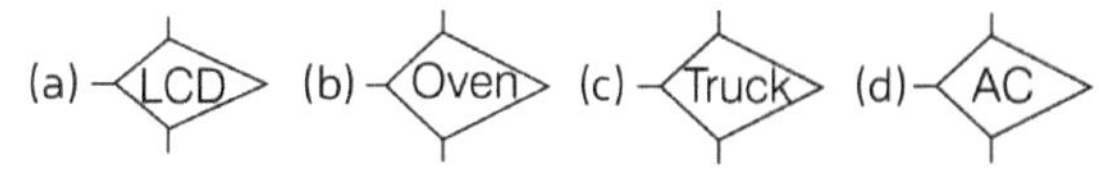

10. Which group of letters does not belong to the group?

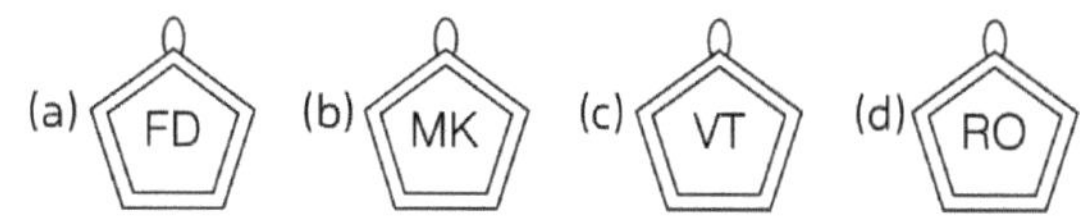

11. Bats and their sizes are given. Find the one which is different.

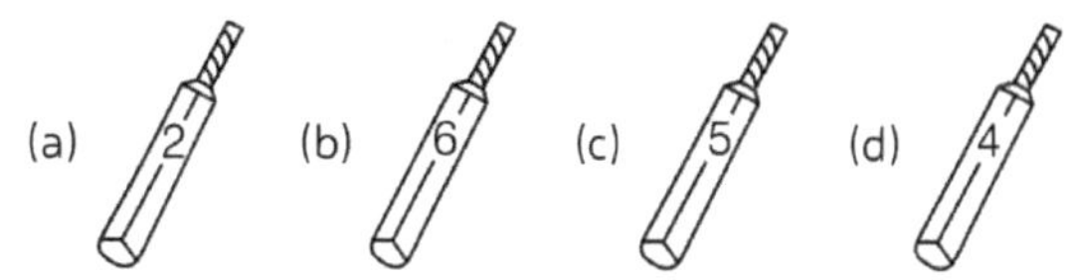

12. From the given alternatives, find a word which is different from others.

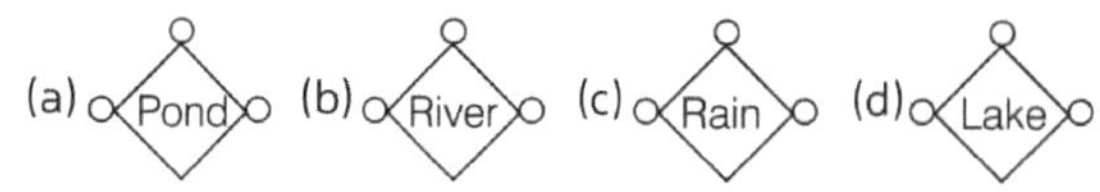

13. Which number does not belong to the group?

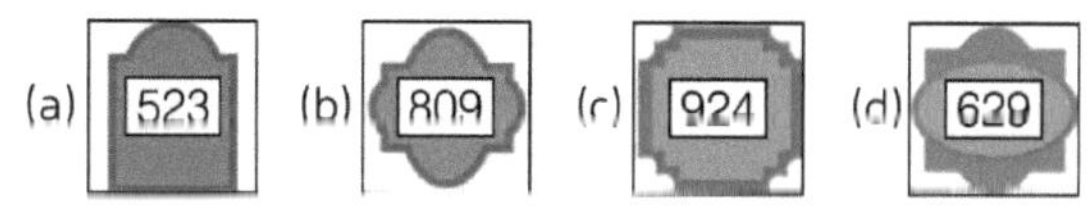

14. Find out the one which is different from others.

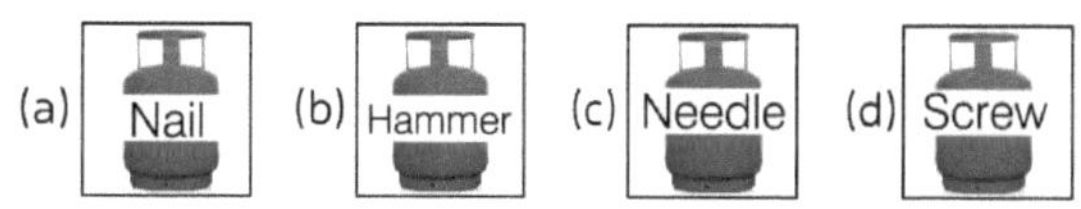

15. Find a number from the given alternatives which is different in the group.

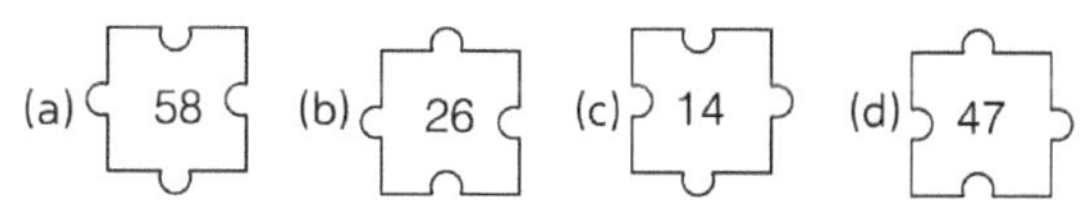

CHAPTER 3

What Comes Next?

In this chapter, questions are asked in which a series consisting of pictures, letters, numbers or patterns is given and it is required to find the term which will continue the series.

Example 1 Below are shown some pictures following a pattern. Based on that find the missing figure.

 ?

(a)

(b)

(c)

(d)

Sol. The first and fifth pictures are same. So, the missing picture should be same as second picture as shown in option (b).

Hence, option (b) is correct.

Example 2 The ice-creams shown below are grouped in patterns 1, 2 and 3. Find the number of ice-creams in pattern 4.

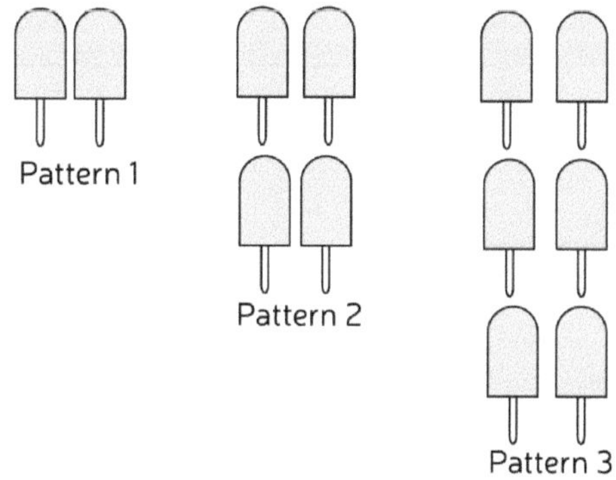

(a) 10 (b) 8 (c) 4 (d) 12

Sol. In pattern 1st, there are 2 ice-creams; in pattern 2nd, there are 4 ice-creams and in pattern 3rd, there are 6 ice-creams. So, the pattern is as follows

$$2 \xrightarrow{+2} 4 \xrightarrow{+2} 6 \xrightarrow{+2} \boxed{8}$$

Thus, there should be 8 ice-creams in pattern 4.

Hence, option (b) is correct.

Example 3 The number series is given below. Find the number that will continue the series.

(a) 17 (b) 20 (c) 18 (d) 15

Sol. The pattern is as follows

$$5 \xrightarrow{+4} 9 \xrightarrow{+4} 13 \xrightarrow{+4} \boxed{17}$$

So, '17' will continue the given series.

Hence, option (a) is correct.

Example 4 Below are given the ice-cream cups. Find the missing letters that should come in place of question mark(?).

(a) (b) (c) (d)

(a) GH (b) EF (c) DE (d) CE

Sol. The pattern is as follows

Ist series, A B C $\boxed{D}$

IInd series, B C D $\boxed{E}$

So, 'DE' should come in place of question mark.

Hence, option (c) is correct.

Let's Practice

1. Which balloon will be the next balloon in the given series?

 ?

(a) 

(b) 

(c) 

(d) 

2. Marie arranges her dolls as follows. Find the doll that will continue the series.

 ?

(a) 

(b) 

(c) 

(d) 

3. Which pattern from the given alternatives will continue the series?

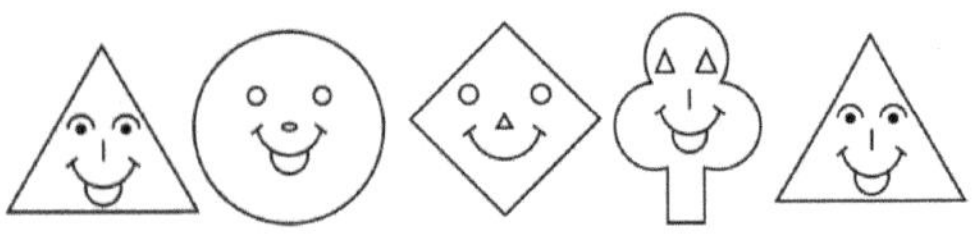 ?

(a) 

(b) 

(c) 

(d) 

4. How many teddies will be there in pattern 5?

Pattern 1 Pattern 2 Pattern 3

(a) 15 (b) 12 (c) 10 (d) 16

5. Which figure will come next in the series shown below?

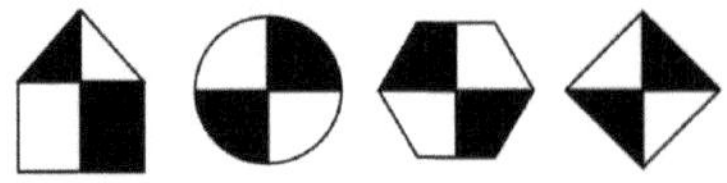 ?

(a) 

(b) 

(c) 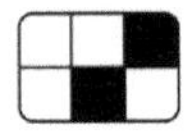

(d) 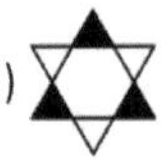

6. Which glass of water should come next in the pattern shown below?

 ?

(a) 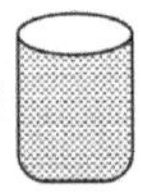

(b) 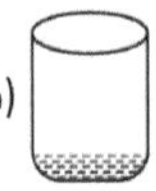

(c) 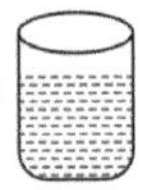

(d) 

7. Identify the pattern followed in the figure and then find the next figure.

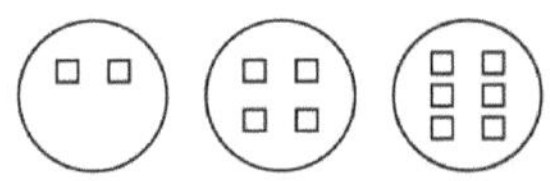 ?

(a) 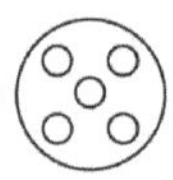

(b) 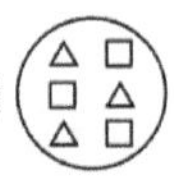

(c) 

(d) 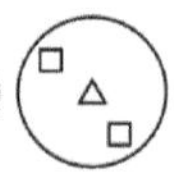

8. Below are given some pictures. Identify the pattern followed by them and then find the missing figure.

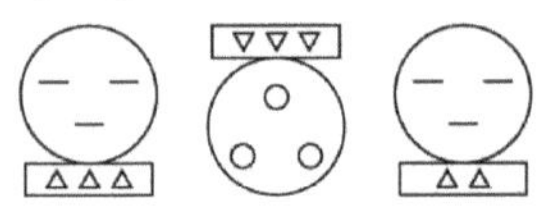 ?

(a) 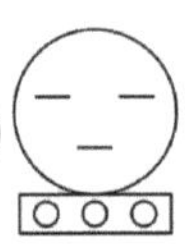

(b) 

(c) 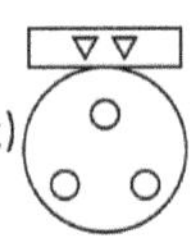

(d) 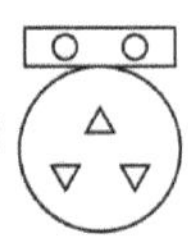

9. Some figures are shown below which follow a certain pattern. Based on that find the figure that will continue the series.

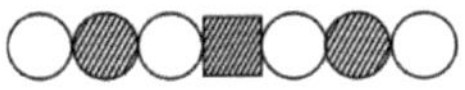

(a)

(b)

(c)

(d)

10. Which number will continue the series shown below?

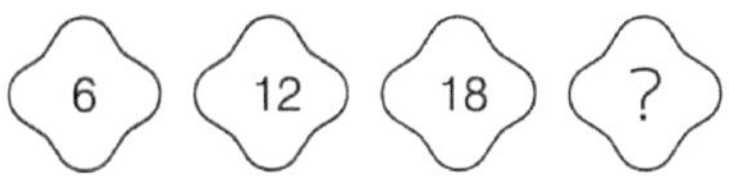

(a) 20
(b) 24
(c) 19
(d) 25

11. In the picture shown below, what should come in place of question mark?

(a) 48
(b) 55
(c) 37
(d) 57

12. Identify the pattern followed in the series shown below and then find the missing number.

(a) 556 (b) 543 (c) 432 (d) 567

13. Which letter will come in the last paper held by the girl?

(a) Q (b) L (c) P (d) N

14. Some letters are written in the pictures shown below following a pattern and form a series. Which letters from the given alternatives will continue the series?

(a) JP (b) TH
(c) QP (d) PG

15. A letters' series is shown below. Find the pair of letters that will continue the series.

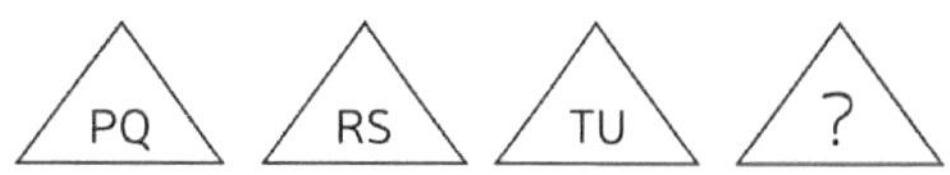

(a) VW (b) XY
(c) WX (d) WY

CHAPTER
4

Let's Decode

In this chapter, figures and letters are coded following a certain rule. In the same manner it is required to find the code for the figure or letters asked in the question.

Example 1 Observe the figures and their codes given below and then answer the question based on it.

Figure	Code	Figure	Code	Figure	Code	Figure	Code
	I		A		C		S

What is the code of  ?

(a) IC (b) IS (c) CA (d) CS

Sol. The code of  is 'I' and the code of  is 'S'.

So, the code of  is 'IS'.

Hence, option (b) is correct.

Example 2 If  is called ,  is called  and  is called , then which vegetable is of purple colour?

(a)  (b)  (c)  (d) 

Sol. The colour of  is purple, but here  is called .

So, the colour of  is purple.

Hence, option (d) is correct.

Example 3 Some letters and their codes are given in the table below.

Letters	A	B	C	D	E	F	G	H	I	J	K	L	M	N	O
Codes	6	p	s	i	@	m	v		2	+	t	–	e	8	x

What is the code of 'MANGO'?

(a) ex6v8 (b) 3+tp@ (c) e68vx (d) @+v8m

Sol. From the given table,

$$M \rightarrow e, A \rightarrow 6, N \rightarrow 8, G \rightarrow v, O \rightarrow x$$

So, the code of 'MANGO' is 'e68vx'.

Hence, option (c) is correct.

Let's Practice

Direction (Q. Nos. 1-3) *Some figures and their codes are shown below. Based on these answer the questions that follow.*

Figures	Codes	Figures	Codes	Figures	Codes
	B		M		T
	G		C		F

1. What is the code of  ?

(a) TM (b) CG (c) BG (d) TF

2. What is the code of  ?

(a) TF (b) CM (c) BF (d) TM

3. What is the code of  ?

(a) TM (b) BF (c) CG (d) CM

Direction (Q. Nos. 4-5) *Some figures and their codes are given below. Answer the questions based on them.*

Figure	Code	Figure	Code	Figure	Code	Figure	Code
	P		G		M		D

4. What is the code of  ?

(a) PD (b) MD
(c) MG (d) DG

5. What is the code of  ?

(a) DG (b) DP (c) PM (d) GM

Direction (Q. Nos. 6-7) *Capital letters from A to Z with their codes are given in the table shown below. Based on the table answer the questions that follow.*

Letters	A	B	C	D	E	F	G	H	I	J	K	L	M
Codes	2	@	0	x	4	i	✡	9	a	b	+	6	g
Letters	N	O	P	q	R	S	T	U	V	W	X	Y	Z
Codes	1	©	e	3	#	h	$	8	7	f		d	5

6. What is the code of PARENT?

(a) f − b + 63 (b) e2#41$
(c) h$x49g (d) c# e12b

7. What is the code of COUNTRY?

(a) +6a1©#h (b) @810$gx
(c) 9✡d4$ f i (d) 0©81$#d

8. If 'Yellow' is called 'Black', 'Black' is called 'Green', 'Green' is called 'Red' and 'Red' is called 'Orange', then what is colour of sky at night?

(a) Green (b) Yellow (c) Red (d) Orange

9. If △ means ○, ○ means □, □ means ▭ and ▭ means ⬠, then which of the following geometrical shapes is ring?

(a) 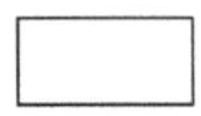 (b) 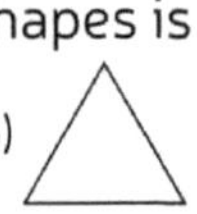 (c) 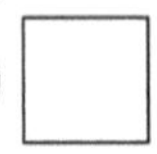 (d) 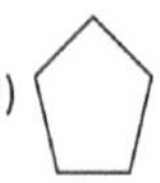

10. If 'Parrot' is called 'Cuckoo, 'Cuckoo' is called 'Peacock', 'Peacock' is called 'Crow' and 'Crow' is called 'Eagle', then which is the national bird of India?

(a) Eagle (b) Parrot (c) Cuckoo (d) Crow

11. If 'Boat' is called 'Car', 'Car' is called 'Scooter' and 'Scooter' is called 'Truck', then which vehicle is two wheeler?

(a) Boat (b) Scooter (c) Truck (d) Car

12. If 'Monday' means 'Tuesday', 'Tuesday' means 'Wednesday' and 'Wednesday' means 'Thursday', then which day is 2nd day after 'Saturday'?

(a) Tuesday (b) Thursday
(c) Monday (d) Wednesday

13. If 'Pencil' means 'Pen', 'Pen' means 'Eraser', 'Eraser' means 'Sharpener' and 'Sharpener' means 'Book', then what is used to erase the text?

(a) Pencil (b) Sharpener (c) Book (d) Pen

14. If 'Agra' is called 'Delhi', 'Delhi' is called 'Mumbai' and 'Mumbai' is called 'Kerala', then what is the capital of India?

(a) Mumbai (b) Delhi (c) Agra (d) Kerala

CHAPTER

5

Alphabet Test

In this chapter, questions are asked from alphabet, i.e. English letters and words.

This chapter, deals with the following questions

- To form meaningful words on filling the following blank space.
- Finding the word, which can or cannot be formed from the letters of the given word.
- Arranging the letters to form meaningful word and also finding their category to which the meaningful word belongs.
- Questions related to letter series.

Example 1 Find the letter from the given alternatives that form two names of birds when replaced with question mark (?).

(a) P
(b) R
(c) D
(d) M

Sol. Letter 'R' will replace the question mark (?) and form two names of birds, which are PARROT and CROW.

Hence, option (b) is correct.

Example 2 Two blocks consisting of two letters are shown below. A block is added between the two blocks having a letter that makes two meaningful words. Find that letter.

(a) M
(b) R
(c) D
(d) T

Sol. Block in between must carry the letter 'T' that makes two meaningful words CAT and TOP.

Hence, option (d) is correct.

Example 3 A banner hanging outside the computer shop is shown below

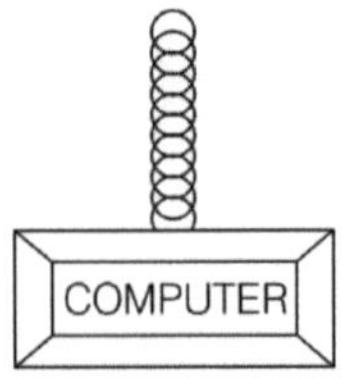

Identify the word from the given alternatives that can be formed using the letters of the word 'COMPUTER'.

(a) TIRE (b) RATE (c) MUTE (d) CART

Sol. 'MUTE' word can be formed using the letters of the word 'COMPUTER'.

Hence, option (c) is correct.

Example 4 Figures shown below consists of letters and numbers below them. Arrange them in a way that they form a meaningful word and find the combination of numbers of the word so formed.

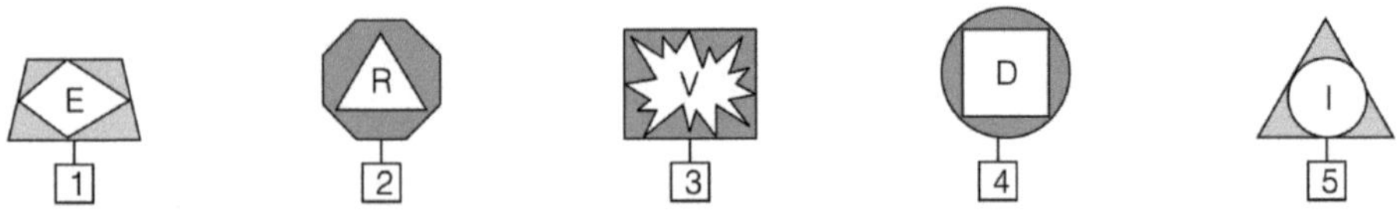

(a) 53412 (b) 12435 (c) 32415 (d) 42531

Sol. After arranging the letters, the meaningful word formed will be 'DRIVE' and the combination of numbers is '42531'.

Hence, option (d) is correct.

Example 5 Four letters are shown below

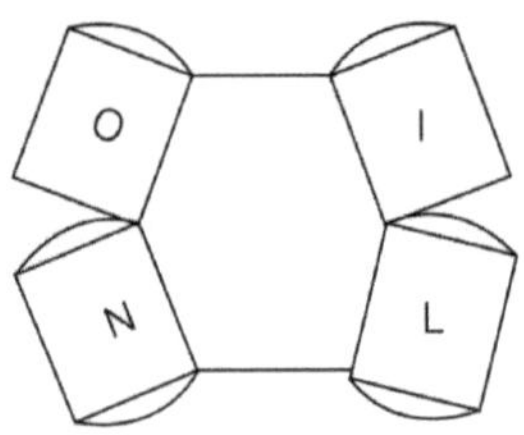

Arrange them in a way that they form a meaningful word and then find its category.

(a) Animal (b) Fruit (c) Flower (d) Vegetable

Sol. The letters when arranged will form a word 'LION', which is an animal.

Hence, option (a) is correct.

Let's Practice

1. Find the letter, which will end the first word and start the second word.

O	N	?	A	T

(a) M (b) R
(c) E (d) L

2. Which letter will end the first word and start the second word?

M A L ? A K E

(a) C (b) E
(c) F (d) L

3. Which letter from the given alternatives when replaced with question mark (?) will form one name of vegetable and one name of fruit?

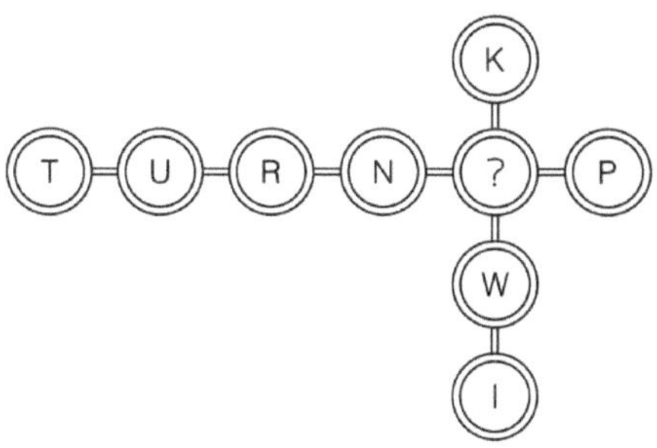

(a) A (b) I
(c) L (d) E

4. Find the letter, which should be replaced with question mark (?) to make the name of two amphibians.

(a) K (b) T
(c) M (d) D

5. Choose the category of the word so formed after arranging the given letters.

(a) Fruit (b) Flower
(c) Cloth (d) Month

6. Identify the category of the word so formed after arranging the given letters.

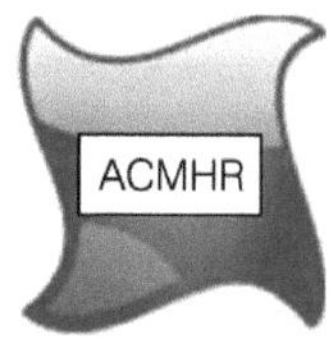

(a) Vegetable (b) Fruit
(c) Flower (d) Month

7. A child holds the following balloons in its hand. Some letters and numbers are written on the balloons. How the letters should be arranged, so that they form a meaningful word? Find the combination of numbers.

(a) 13215 (b) 24351
(c) 13245 (d) 31452

8. Choose the correct combination of numbers, so that letters when arranged form a meaningful word.

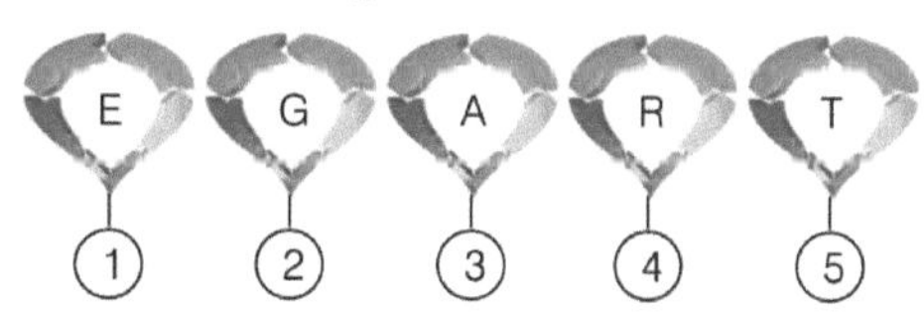

(a) 43125 (b) 24135
(c) 31254 (d) 54321

9. Choose the word from the given alternatives, which can be formed using the letters of the given word.

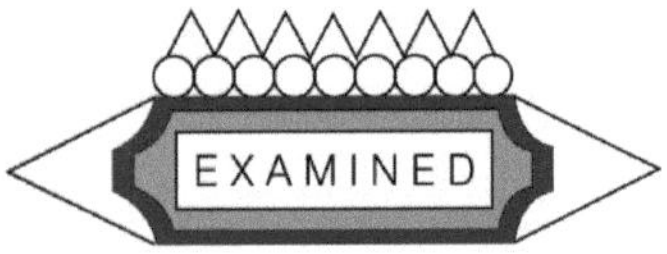

(a) EXTRA (b) NEXT
(c) MIND (d) MINT

10. Find the word from the given alternatives, which can be formed using the letters of the given word.

(a) GATE (b) LATE
(c) TALE (d) GOAL

11. Identify the word, which cannot be formed using the letters of the given word.

(a) HEAL (b) REAL
(c) GAME (d) LATER

12. Which word from the given alternatives cannot be formed using the letters of the given word?

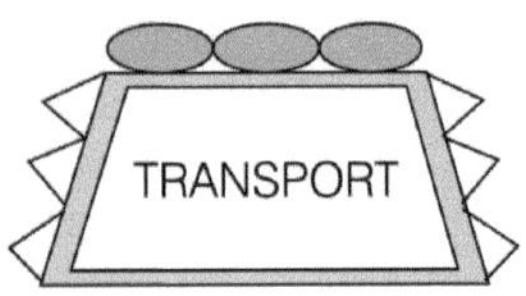

(a) SPORT
(b) TRUST
(c) STRAP
(d) START

Direction (Q. Nos. 13-15) *Observe the given letter series carefully and answer the questions that follow.*

A B C D E F G H I J K L M Z Y X W V U T S R Q P O N
(Left end) (Right end)

13. Which letter is fifteenth from the left end?
(a) Y
(b) L
(c) G
(d) W

14. How many letters are there between I and X?
(a) 5
(b) 4
(c) 8
(d) 6

15. If all vowels are removed from above letter series, then which letter comes just after V?
(a) U
(b) V
(c) X
(d) T

16. If in the work 'DISTURBANCE' the first letter is interchanged with the last letter, the second letter is interchanged with the tenth letter and so on, which letter would come after the letter T in the newly formed word?
(a) S (b) I
(b) T (d) N

17. How many meaningful words can be formed with the letters ESRO using each letter only once in each word?
(a) None (b) One
(c) Two (d) Three

CHAPTER 6

Finding Positions

There are four positions, which can be understood with the help of the given diagram.

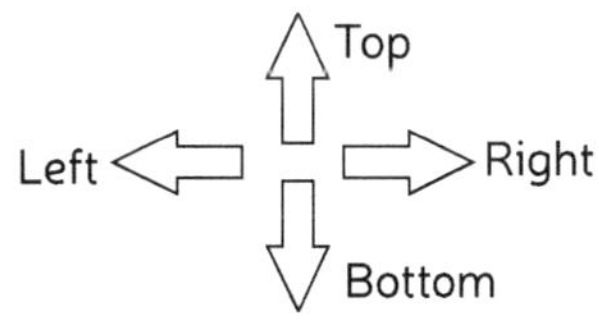

Types of questions covered in this chapter are as follow

- Finding the position of an object from left, right, top or bottom.
- Find the object after interchanging the positions or removing of objects from the given sequence.

Direction (Ex. Nos. 1-2) *In a toy shop some identical toy dolls are kept in a way as shown below. Observe them and answer the questions that follow.*

Example 1 Doll E is at what position from the left end?

(a) 4th (b) 5th (c) 3th (d) 6th

Example 2 Doll B is at what position from the right end?

(a) 6th (b) 7th (c) 3rd (d) 5th

Solution (Ex. Nos. 1-2)

1. It is clear from the given arrangement of dolls that doll E is at 5th position from the left end.

   A B C D E F G
   Left ⟶ Right
   5th

   Hence, option (b) is correct.

2. Position of doll B from the right end is 6th when we count from the right, i.e. from doll G to doll B.

   A B C D E F G
   Left ⟵ Right
   6th

   Hence, option (a) is correct.

   Note If end positions are not marked, then by default the positions are taken from our side.

Direction (Ex. Nos. 3-4) *Observe the position of the toffees carefully and answer the questions based on them.*

1 2 3 4 5 6 7

Example 3 If toffee 3 is removed from the row, then how many toffees are there between toffee 2 and toffee 6?

(a) 4 (b) 5 (c) 2 (d) 3

Example 4 If the positions of toffee 2 and toffee 5 are interchanged, then which toffee is second to the left of toffee 2?

(a) 5 (b) 3 (c) 6 (d) 1

Solution (Ex. Nos. 3-4)

3. There are two toffees between toffee 2 and toffee 6 when toffee 3 is removed and this can be shown as

   Left 1 2 ~~3~~ [4 5] 6 7 Right

   So, 4 and 5 will be between toffee 2 and toffee 6.

   Hence, option (c) is correct.

4. When toffee 2 and toffee 5 interchange its positions, then the positions of toffees can be shown as

   Left 1 5 [3] 4 2 6 7 Right
   ⟵ 2nd to the left

   So, toffee 3 is second to the left of toffee 2.

   Hence, option (b) is correct.

Example 5 In a race of four boys, Tany is ahead of stephen, but behind Harper. Harper is between Jack and Tany. Who amongst the four won the race?

(a) Stephen (b) Tany (c) Harper (d) Jack

Sol. The positions of the four participants can be shown as

From the above positions of the boys, we see that Jack won the race.

Hence, option (d) is correct.

Let's Practice

1. Some similar toys are hanging in a toy shop which are shown below.

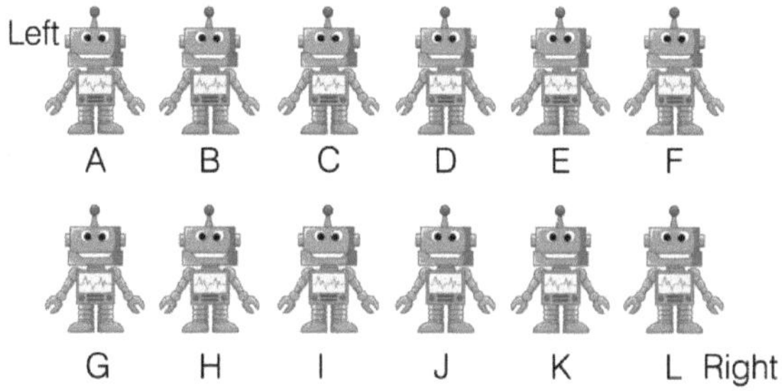

Which toy is hanging fifth to the left of toy I?

(a) E (b) D
(c) C (d) G

2. Seven books are arranged in a shelf as shown below and given the name as K, L, M, N, O, P and Q. If book M is at third position from the top, then what is its position from the bottom?

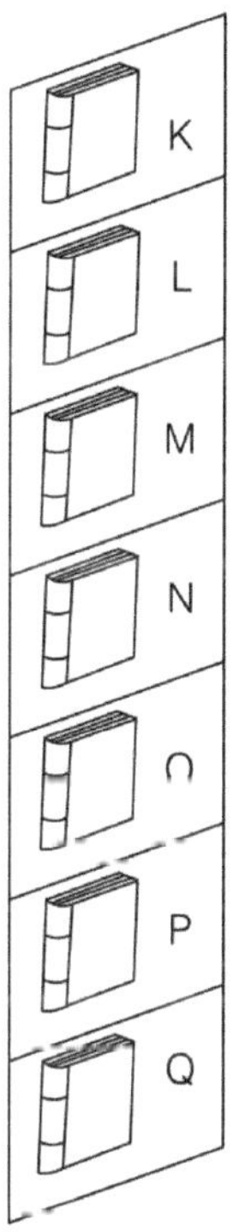

(a) 4th (b) 6th
(c) 5th (d) 3rd

Direction (Q. Nos. 3-4) *Some trees are planted in a garden as shown below and named as P, Q, R, S, T, U and V. Now, answer the questions based on their positions.*

3. Tree S is between tree R and tree

(a) Q (b) T
(c) U (d) P

4. Which tree is fourth to the right of tree Q?

(a) S (b) T
(c) U (d) V

5. Some teddies are drawn on a wall as shown below and the letters represent their names. If the positions of F and J are interchanged, then which teddy is second to the left of F?

(a) G (b) H
(c) E (d) K

Direction (Q. Nos. 6-7) *Observe the given pictures carefully and answer the questions based on it.*

6. How many boys are behind the boy on 4th position?

(a) 6 (b) 7
(c) 5 (d) 3

7. If boys on 2nd and 8th positions interchange their positions, then who is third to the right of 8th boy after interchanging the position?

(a) 2nd boy (b) 4th boy
(c) 5th boy (d) 9th boy

Direction (Q. Nos. 8-9) *Look at the arrangement of teddies and answer the questions that follow.*

8. Which teddy is at 5th position from the right end?

(a) B (b) C
(c) E (d) D

9. If teddy F is removed from the arrangement, then which teddy is to the immediate left of teddy G?

(a) C
(b) D
(c) B
(d) E

10. If flowers 3 and 9 are removed from the arrangement, then how many flowers are there between 5th and 10th flower?

(a) 2
(b) 4
(c) 3
(d) 5

Direction (Q. Nos. 11-12) *Nine ice-cream cones are kept in a stand as shown below. Answer the questions based on their positions.*

11. If one more ice-cream cone N is kept in a stand after M, then how many ice-cream cones are to the left of cone J?

(a) 5 (b) 7
(c) 6 (d) 3

12. If two ice-cream cones G and M are removed from stand, then which cone is in the middle of the stand?

(a) K (b) H
(c) J (d) I

13. Emme, Ela, Bryan and Tina measure their weights. Ela is heavier than Tina but lighter than Bryan. Bryan is lighter than only Emme. Who is heaviest among all?

(a) Bryan (b) Ela
(c) Emme (d) Tina

14. Four friends started measuring their heights by a measuring tape. Rafael's height was more than Maria, but he was shorter than Novak. Novak does not have the maximum height amongst the four friends. Mike's height is more than Maria. Who amongst them is the smallest?

(a) Rafael (b) Novak
(c) Mike (d) Maria

15. In an examination, Bob scored more than only Andy. Harry scored more than Peter. Who scored highest marks among these four?

(a) Bob (b) Harry
(c) Peter (d) Andy

CHAPTER 7

Directions

There are four main directions, whose names are East, West, North and South, which can be easily understood with the help of adjacent diagram.

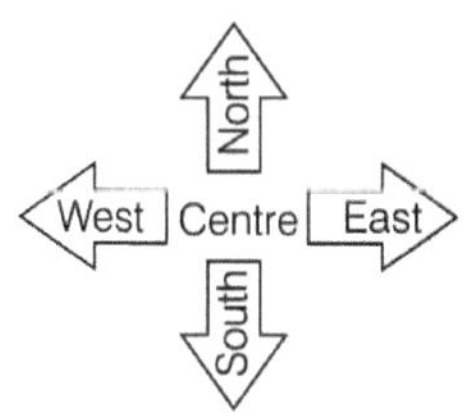

Direction (Ex. Nos. 1-2) *Observe the positions of the trees in the garden and answer the questions that follow.*

Example 1 Which tree is in the East direction?

(a) Mango tree (b) Apple tree (c) Banana tree (d) Coconut tree

Example 2 Banana tree is in which direction in the garden?

(a) West (b) North (c) East (d) South

Solution (Ex. Nos. 1-2) The position of trees can be shown as

Coconut tree (North)

Mango tree (West) Centre Apple tree (East)

Banana tree (South)

1. From the above diagram it is clear that, apple tree is in the East direction. Hence, option (b) is correct.
2. From the above diagram it is clear that, banana tree is in the South direction according to its position in the garden.
   Hence, option (d) is correct.

Let's Practice

Direction (Q. Nos. 1-2) *Observe the positions of House, Church, Grocery shop and Temple and then answer the questions that follow.*

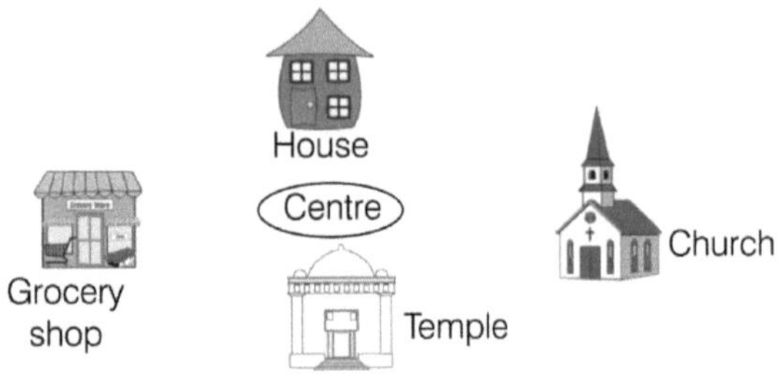

1. House is in which direction from the temple?
   (a) North (b) East (c) South (d) West

2. Which place is in the West direction?
   (a) House (b) Church
   (c) Grocery shop (d) Temple

Direction (Q. Nos. 3-4) *Observe the positions of toys kept in a toy shop and then answer the questions that follow.*

3. Cat is in which direction from monkey?
   (a) North (b) West (c) South (d) East

4. Which toy is in the North direction?
   (a) Kitty (b) Monkey (c) Cat (d) Elephant

Direction (Q. Nos. 5-6) *Four items are shown below. Observe them and then answer the questions based on them.*

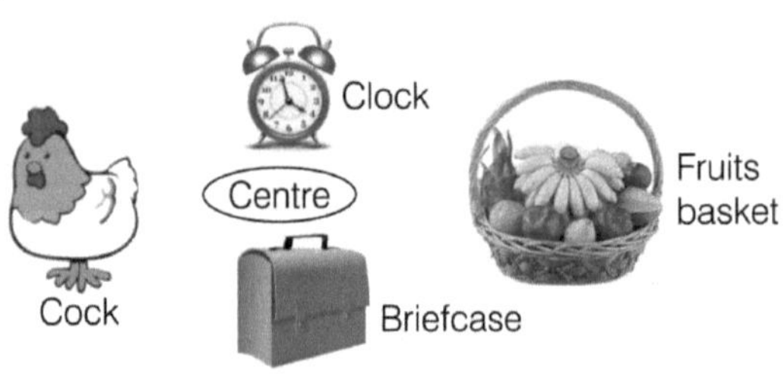

5. Which item is in the West direction?
   (a) Fruits basket
   (b) Clock
   (c) Briefcase
   (d) Cock

6. Clock is in which direction from the briefcase?
   (a) North (b) East (c) South (d) West

Direction (Q. Nos. 7-8) *Read the map of India shown below and then answer the questions that follow.*

7. Which place is in the South direction in the above map?
   (a) Madhya Pradesh (b) Bihar
   (c) Punjab (d) Kerala

8. Gujarat is in which direction from Jharkhand?
   (a) West (b) South (c) East (d) North

Direction (Q. Nos. 9-10) *Tom, Julia, Martin and Harry are playing a game and standing as shown below. Answer the questions asked based on their positions.*

9. Martin is standing in which direction?
   (a) North (b) East (c) South (d) West

10. Who is standing in the East direction?
    (a) Harry (b) Julia (c) Tom (d) Martin

CHAPTER

8

Pattern Completion

Pattern completion means completing the given pattern which can be in geometrical form or a number pattern following some rule.

Example 1 A block consists of the shapes which follow a certain pattern. Following the same pattern, find the missing figure in the block.

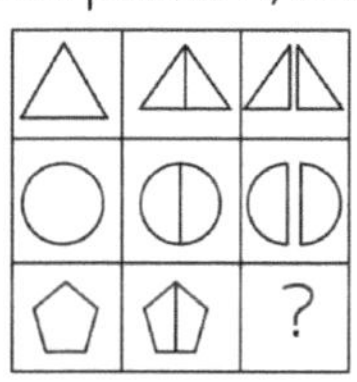

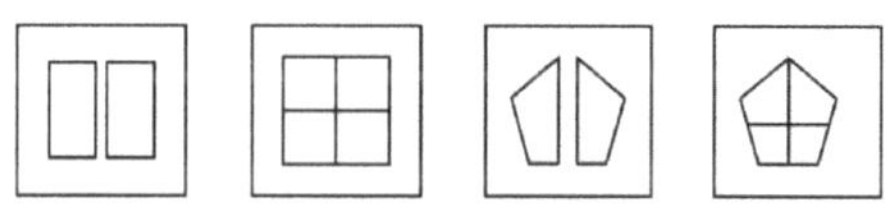

(a) (b) (c) (d)

Sol. In each row a pattern is followed. A line is drawn in the middle of first shape of the row to get the second shape. Then, the second shape is separated along the line to get the third shape. So, figure in option (c) is the missing figure.

Hence, option (c) is correct.

Example 2 A child has following shapes on which numbers are written. He combines them to form a pattern and get a number. Following the same rule, find the missing number.

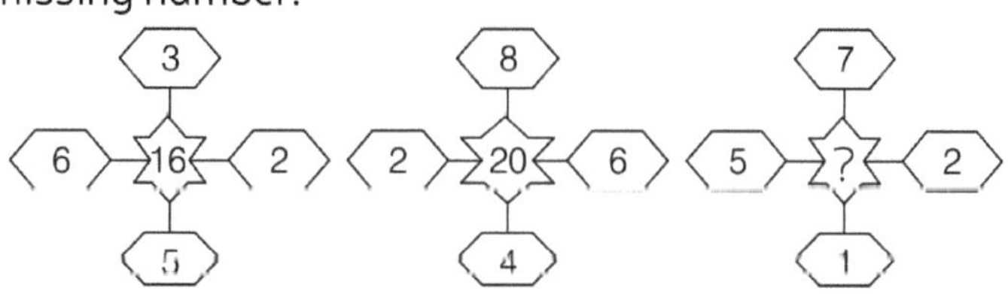

(a) 17 (b) 15 (c) 12 (d) 10

Sol. The pattern is as follows

$$3+2+5+6=16,\ 8+6+4+2=20 \text{ and } 7+2+1+5=\boxed{15}$$

So, '15' is the missing number.

Hence, option (b) is correct.

Let's Practice

1. Choose the figure from the given alternatives that will complete the given pattern.

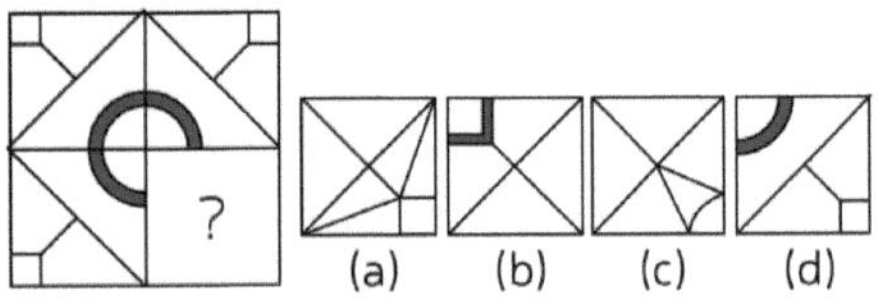

2. A cloth consists of the following pattern from which a part is missing. Find that missing part of the pattern.

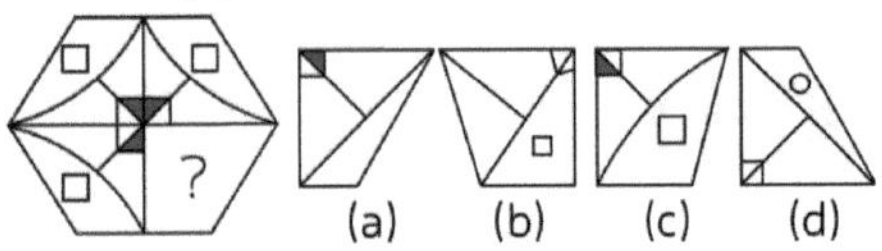

3. Identify the figure from the options that will complete the given pattern.

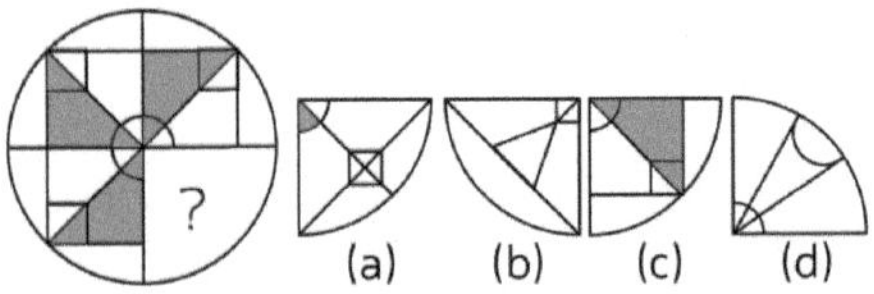

4. Which of the following options will complete the given pattern?

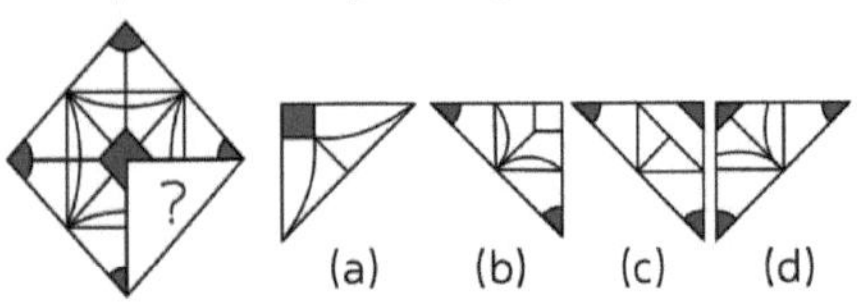

5. Find the missing number from the given options.

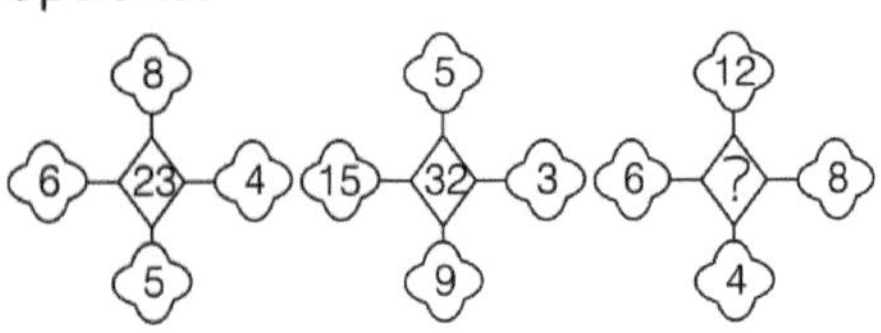

(a) 25 (b) 30 (c) 35 (d) 40

6. Choose the missing number from the given alternatives.

(a) 48 (b) 27 (c) 42 (d) 40

7. Tom draws the following shapes and writes some numbers in it. Find the missing number follow the same rule.

(a) 63 (b) 54 (c) 49 (d) 56

8. Which number will replace the question mark (?) in the given pattern?

(a) 6
(b) 5
(c) 7
(d) 4

9. The given block consists of numbers and these numbers follow a certain rule. Follow the same rule and find the missing number.

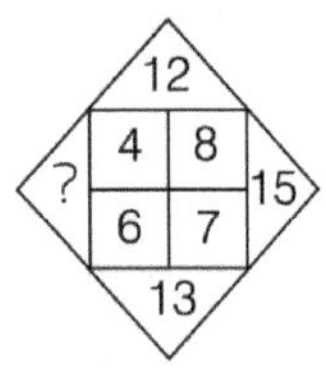

(a) 12
(b) 9
(c) 8
(d) 10

10. Find the missing number from the given alternatives.

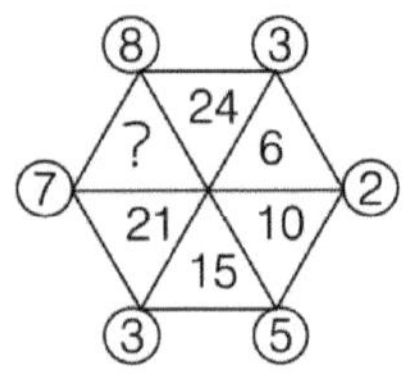

(a) 56
(b) 54
(c) 42
(d) 50

11. The shape given below is having numbers inside and outside it. What number from the given options will replace the question mark(?)?

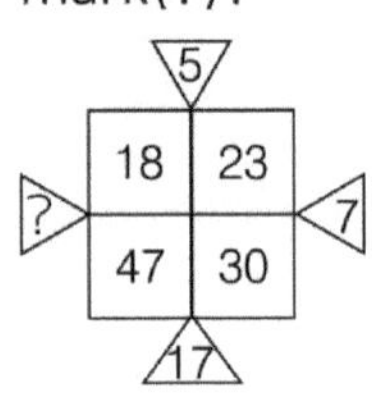

(a) 25
(b) 24
(c) 29
(d) 20

12. A pattern on a bedsheet consists of the following figures. Find the missing figure in the pattern.

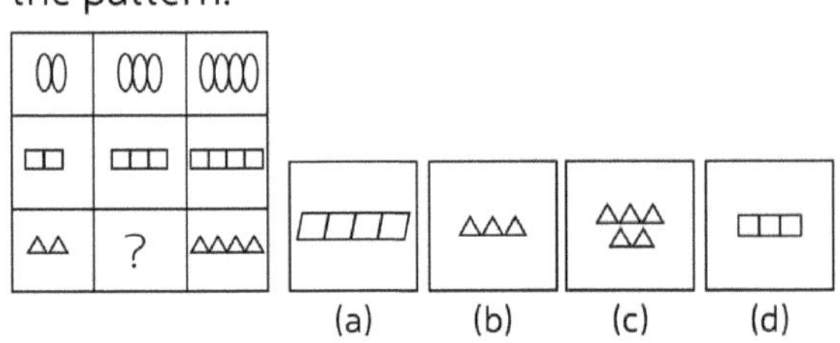

CHAPTER

9

Mirror Images

In 'Mirror image', the left part of an object appears right and right part appears left in a mirror.

Example 1 Andy kept his elephant toy in front of the mirror. How will it look like in the mirror?

(X) (a) (b) (c) (d)

Sol. The correct mirror image of the elephant toy is given in option (d) as shown in adjoining figure.

Hence, option (d) is correct.

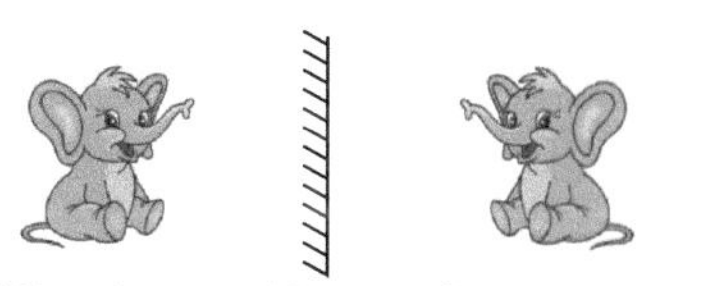

Mirror image Mirror Original image

Example 2 A decorated lamp is hanging in a house. Which one will be its mirror image?

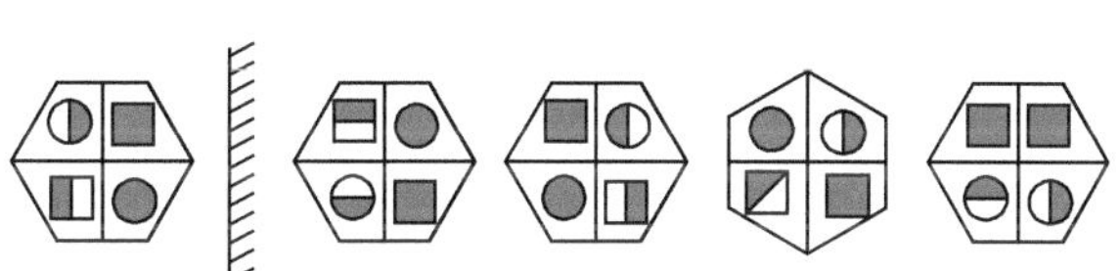

(X) (a) (b) (c) (d)

Sol. The correct mirror image of the decorated lamp is as shown in adjoining figure.

Hence, option (b) is correct.

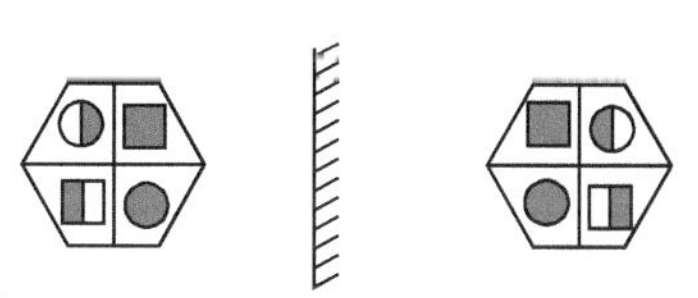

Original image Mirror Mirror image

Example 3 The given below numbers are written on a wall. The mirror image of the numbers will be

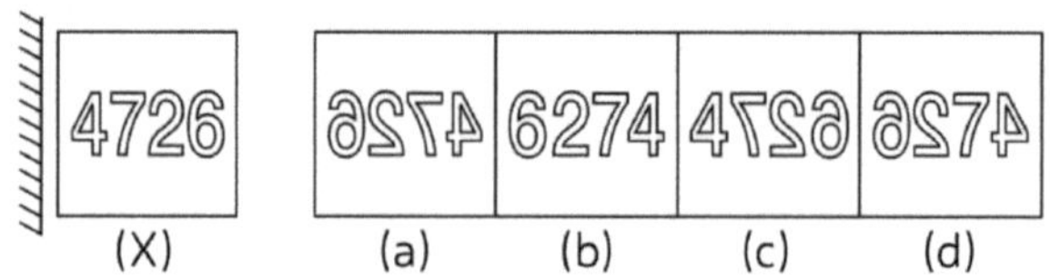

Sol. First of all we will observe the mirror image of numbers.

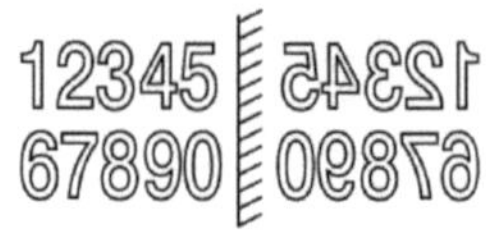

The correct mirror image of the numbers is given in option (a) as shown below

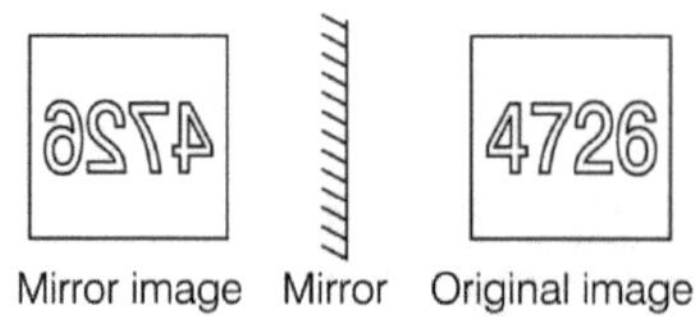

Hence, option (a) is correct.

Example 4 Four letters are written outside a shop. How the letters will appear in the side mirror of the car?

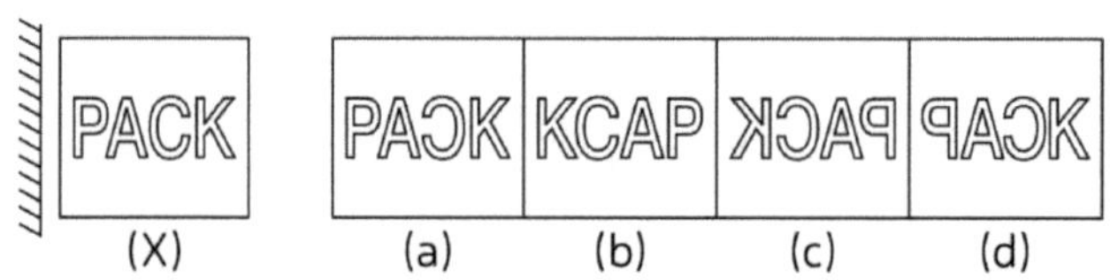

Sol. First of all we will observe the mirror image of letters.

The four letters will appear in the side mirror of the car as given in option (c) as shown below

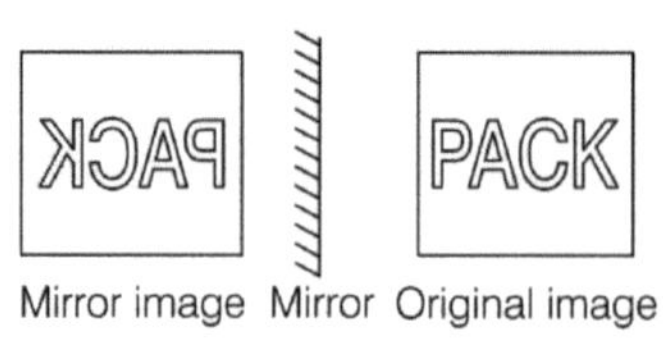

Hence, option (c) is correct.

Let's Practice

1. A picture is drawn on a cardboard. What will be its mirror image?

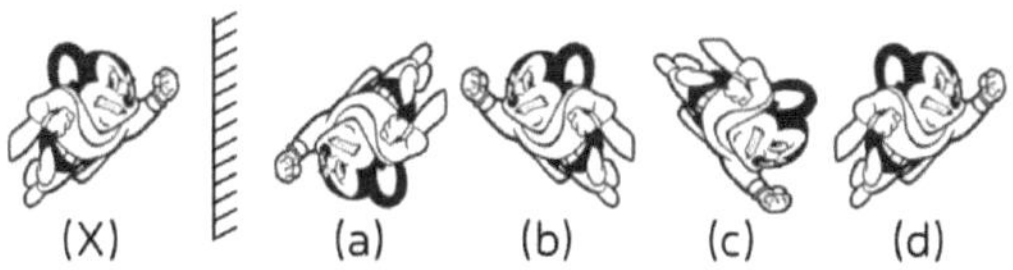

2. Choose the correct mirror image of a dog standing beside the mirror.

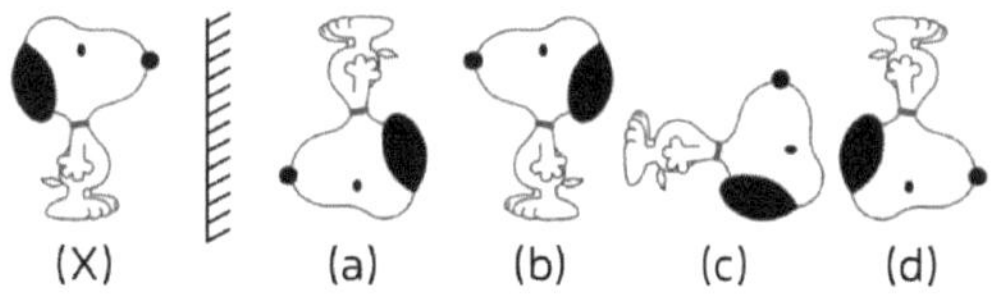

3. Jake's photograph as shown below is kept on a table. What will be the mirror image of the photograph?

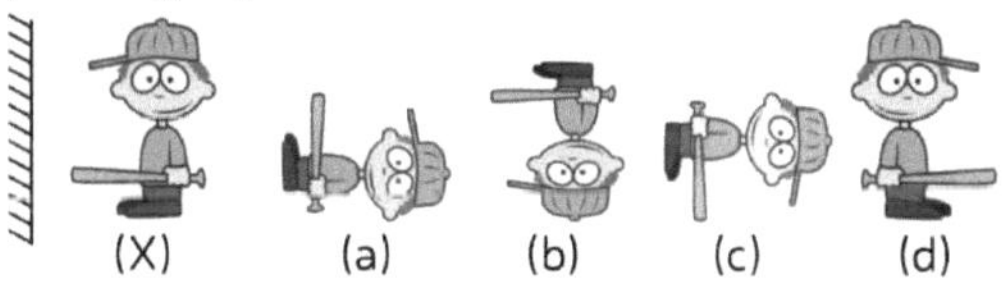

4. A child kept a toy in front of the mirror as shown below. How will it appear in the mirror?

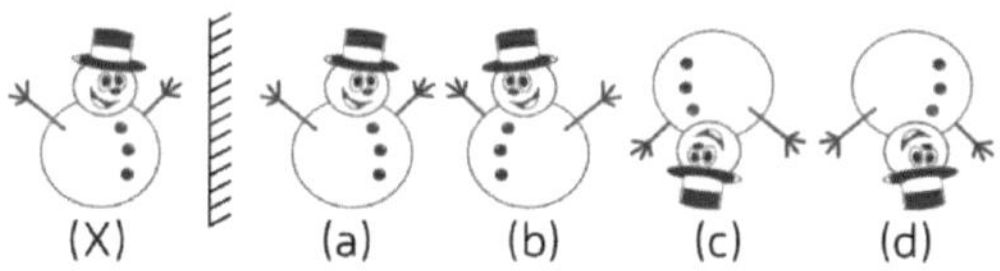

5. What will be the mirror image of kitty?

6. Find the correct mirror image of the figure shown below.

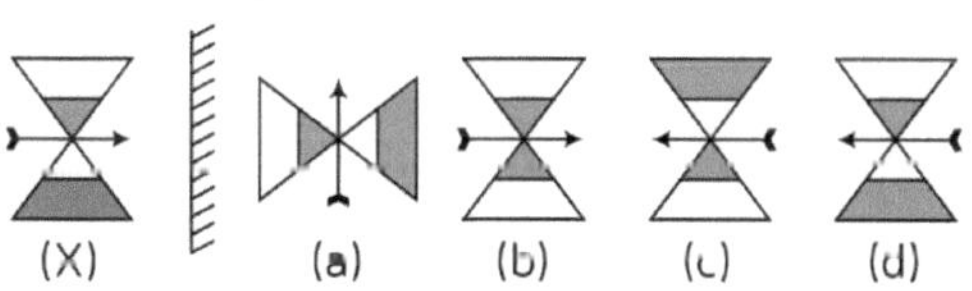

7. Harry is holding a block in his hand that is given. What will be the mirror image of the block?

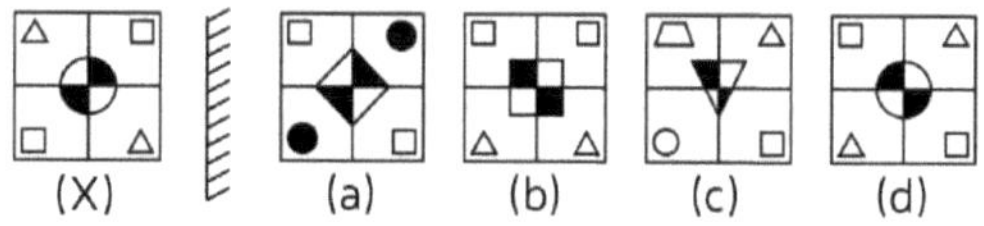

8. Choose the correct mirror image of the pattern shown below.

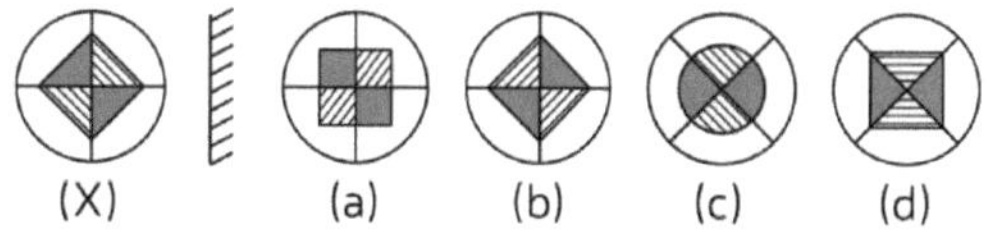

9. Choose the correct mirror image of the block shown below.

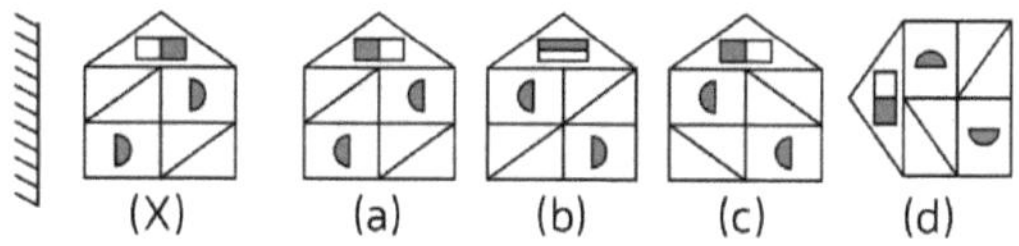

10. Find the mirror image of the numbers shown by the electronic meter.

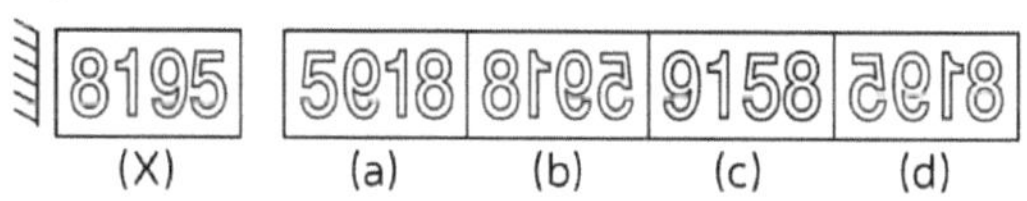

11. Find the correct mirror image of the numbers.

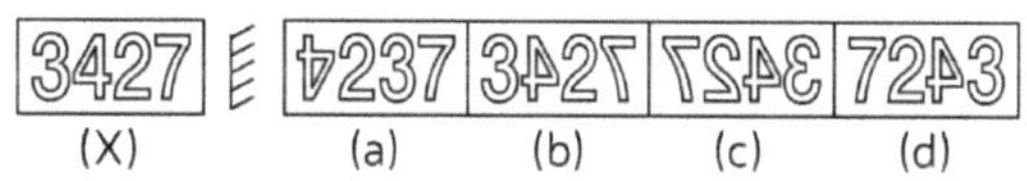

12. Three letters are written on a T-shirt, a man is wearing. How will the letters appear when that man stands in front of the mirror?

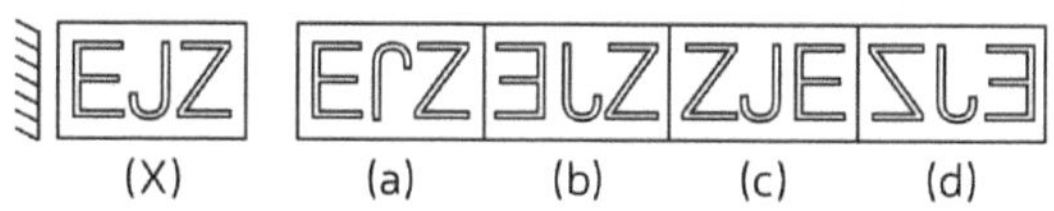

13. The word written on the wall outside a shop is shown below. What will be its mirror image?

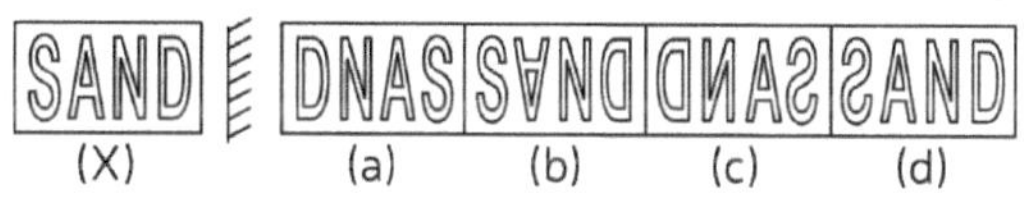

14. The code of a product is depicted on it. Find its mirror image from the given options.

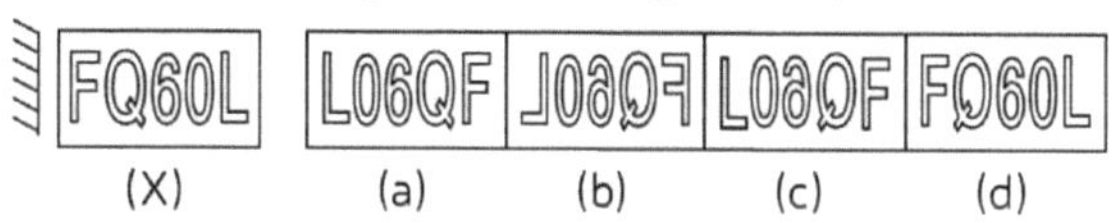

CHAPTER 10

Hidden Figures

This chapter includes questions of two types. First is, finding the given part in the option figures and, second is, finding which part from the options is hidden in the given figure.

Example 1 Lina draws a figure on a piece of paper and finds that the figure exists in any of the given pictures shown below. Find the picture in which the given part is hidden.

(a)  (b)  (c)  (d) 

Sol. The given part is hidden in option (c) as shown in adjacent figure.
Hence, option (c) is correct.

Example 2 A pattern is made on a fibre sheet as shown below. Find a figure from the options which is exactly hidden in the given pattern.

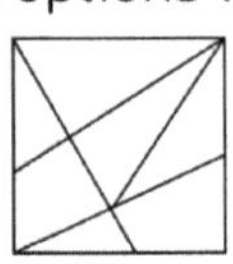

(a)  (b) 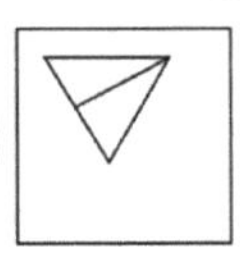 (c) 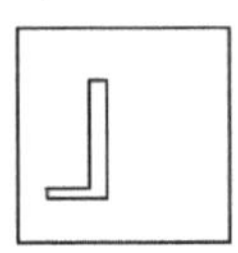 (d) 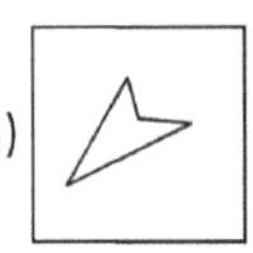

Sol. Figure in option (b) is exactly hidden in the given pattern as shown in adjacent figure.
Hence, option (b) is correct.

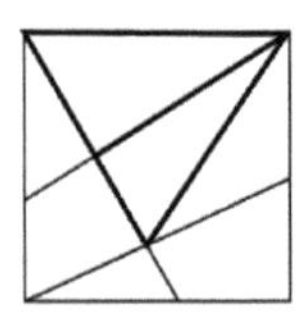

Let's Practice

1. In which of the following pictures the given shape (X) is hidden?

(X) (a) (b) (c) (d)

2. Look at the shape shown below and find the picture from the options in which it is hidden.

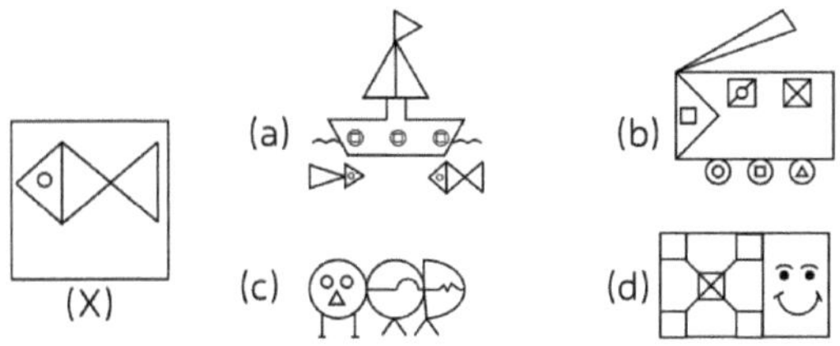

(X) (a) (b) (c) (d)

3. Dany finds a missing part of a toy as shown below. Find the toy to which this part belongs.

(X) (a) (b) (c) (d)

4. Identify the figure from the given options in which the given shape (X) is hidden.

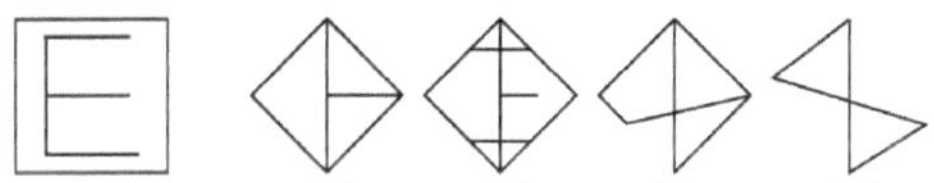

(X) (a) (b) (c) (d)

5. Find the figure from the given options in which the given shape (X) is hidden.

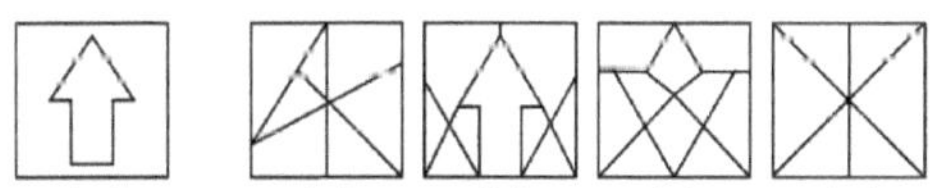

(X) (a) (b) (c) (d)

6. In which of the following figures, the given shape (X) is hidden as one of its part?

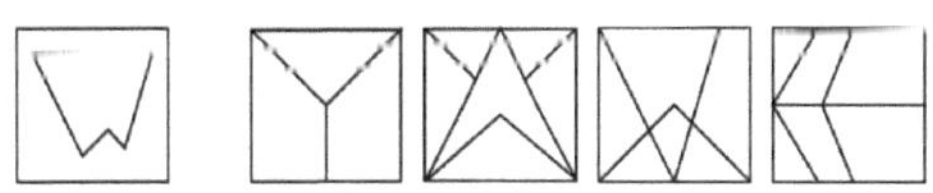

(X) (a) (b) (c) (d)

7. Luca draws a shape on a sheet of paper. Find in which of the following figures the given shape (X) is hidden.

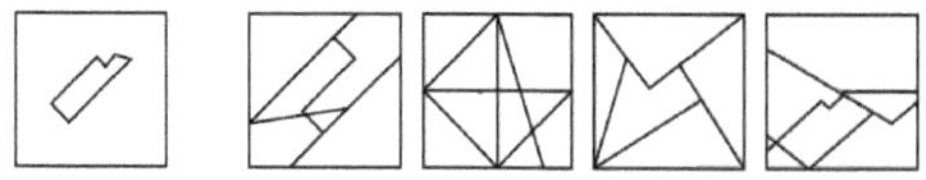

(X) (a) (b) (c) (d)

8. A part of the main figure is shown below. Find the figure from the options to which it belongs.

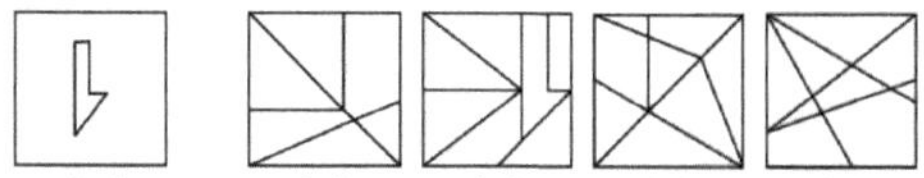

(X) (a) (b) (c) (d)

9. Below is given a triangle shaped pattern. Find from the options, which figure is hidden in the triangle shaped pattern.

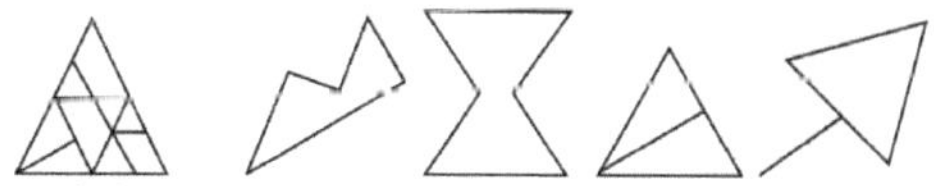

(X) (a) (b) (c) (d)

10. Identify the figure from the options which is hidden in figure (X).

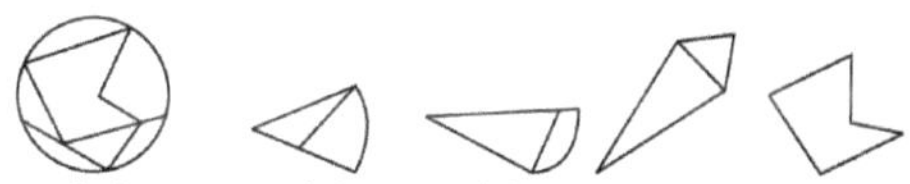

(X) (a) (b) (c) (d)

11. Which figure from the given options is hidden in the figure (X)?

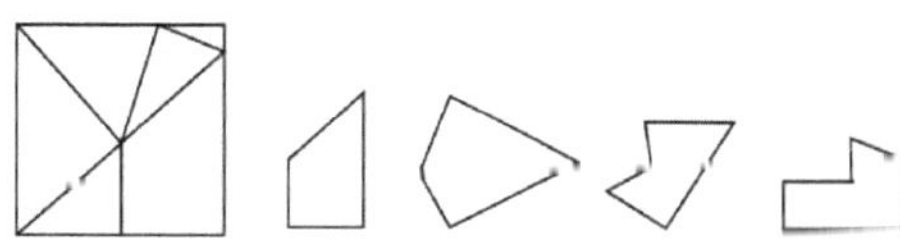

(X) (a) (b) (c) (d)

12. A book's front cover consists of the following figures as shown below. Find a figure from the given options, which is hidden in the figure shown below.

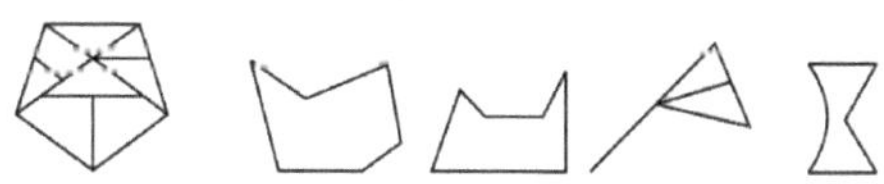

(X) (a) (b) (c) (d)

CHAPTER 11

Geometrical Shapes

In this chapter, some figures are given and it is asked to count the number of lines, circles, triangles, squares, etc.

Geometrical shapes include line, circle, triangle etc.

Let us observe some geometrical shapes.

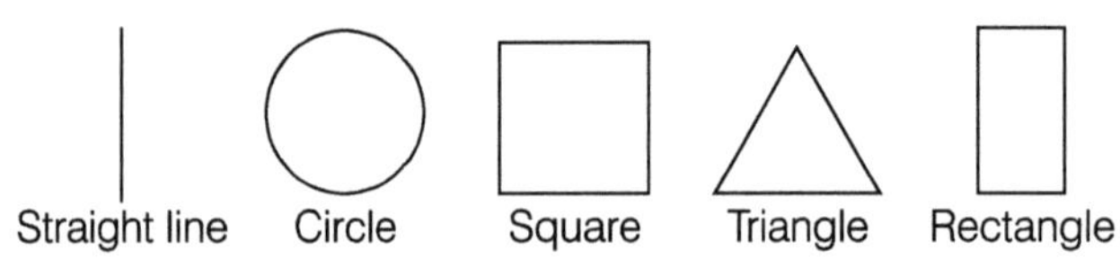

Example 1 A figure shown below is drawn on a wall. Find the number of straight lines in the given figure.

(a) 12 (b) 14 (c) 10 (d) 8

Sol. The figure can be labelled as shown below

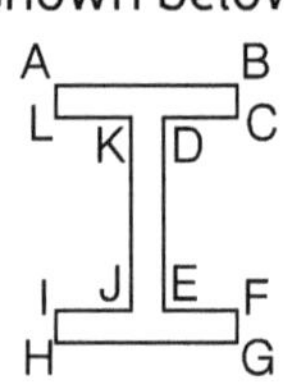

Number of straight lines = AB, BC, CD, DE, EF, FG, GH, HI, IJ, JK, KL and AL = 12

Hence, option (a) is correct.

Direction (Ex. Nos. 2-3) *Look at the picture given below and answer the questions that follow.*

Example 2 Find the number of circles in the given picture.

(a) 10 (b) 12 (c) 8 (d) 14

Example 3 Count the number of rectangles in the given picture.

(a) 8 (b) 10 (c) 13 (d) 11

Solution (Ex. Nos. 2-3) *The given picture can be labelled as shown below*

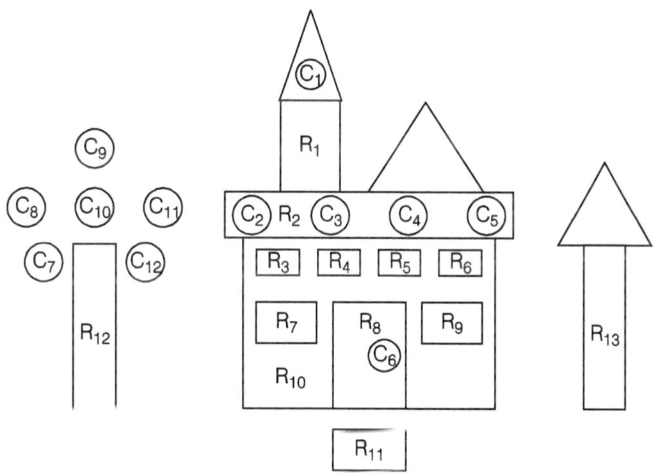

2. Number of circles in the above picture is 12.
   Hence, option (b) is correct.
3. Number of rectangles in the above picture is 13.
   Hence, option (c) is correct.

Let's Practice

1. A child is climbing the stairs as shown in the picture. Find the number of straight lines in it.

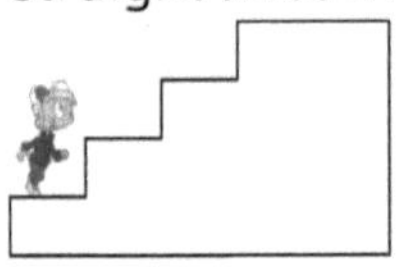

(a) 8
(b) 12
(c) 10
(d) 11

2. Count the different types of closed shapes in the given picture.

(a) 3
(b) 4
(c) 5
(d) 6

3. In the X-mas tree, how many slant lines are there?

(a) 3
(b) 4
(c) 5
(d) 6

4. From the given picture count the number of triangles.

(a) 5
(b) 8
(c) 4
(d) 3

5. Tany looks at the following picture and observes the different types of shapes. How many types of shapes are there in the picture?

(a) 6 (b) 3 (c) 5 (d) 4

6. A picture is shown below. Find the number of circles in it.

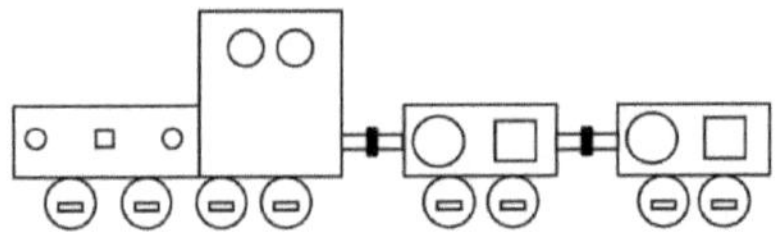

(a) 18 (b) 16 (c) 14 (d) 15

7. Count the number of rectangles and triangles in the picture shown below.

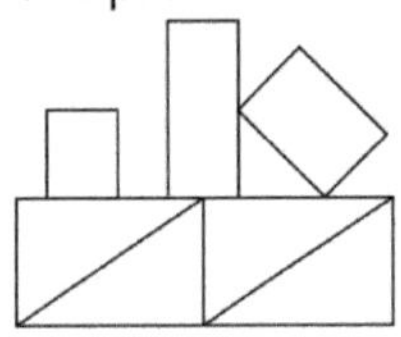

(a) 6, 5
(b) 5, 4
(c) 6, 7
(d) 7, 6

8. Select the correct shape used to form solids.

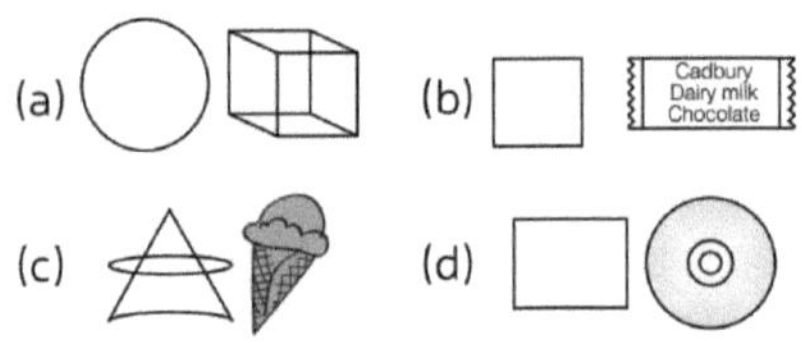

9. In the given picture, count the number of circles.

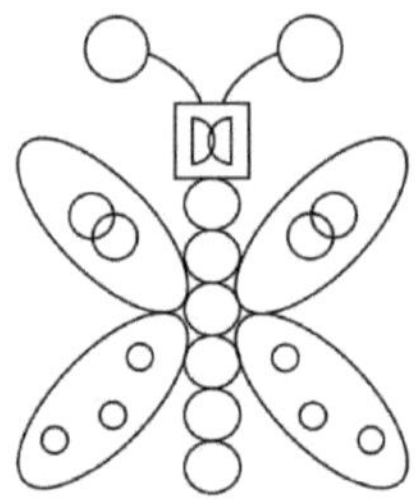

(a) 15 (b) 18
(c) 10 (d) 12

10. A kite is kept on the floor. Find the number of triangles in it.

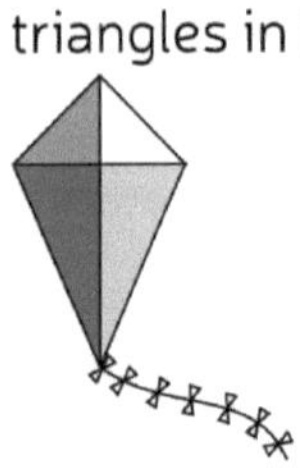

(a) 22 (b) 20
(c) 18 (d) 15

11. Find the number of rectangles in the given picture hanging on a wall.

(a) 6
(b) 7
(c) 8
(d) 5

Direction (Q. Nos. 12-13) *Look at the picture shown below and answer the questions that follow.*

12. Count the number of rectangles in the picture.
(a) 8 (b) 10 (c) 9 (d) 11

13. Find the number of squares in the picture.
(a) 5 (b) 7 (c) 8 (d) 10

Direction (Q. Nos. 14-15) *Look at the following picture and answer the questions given below.*

14. Find the number of triangles in the given picture.
(a) 12 (b) 13 (c) 14 (d) 15

15. What is the difference between the number of triangles and number of circles in the given picture?
(a) 2 (b) 5 (c) 8 (d) 4

Practice Set 1

A Test Based on the Whole Content

1. Identify the one that does not belong to the group.
(a) Friday (b) Monday (c) Wednesday (d) Today

2. Figures in the first pair are related to each other in a certain way. Find the missing figure in the second pair in the same way as the first pair.

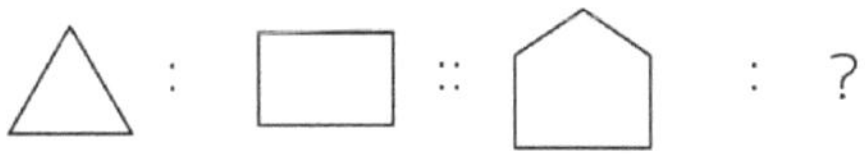

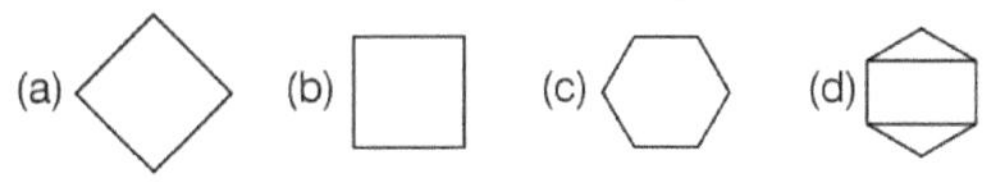

3. Which letter from the given alternatives will complete the first word and start the second word.

D – A – G – ? – A – C – H

(a) S (b) T (c) E (d) R

4. If Black is called Pink, Pink is called Yellow, Yellow is called Red, Red is called Blue, then what is the colour of Sunflower?
(a) Red (b) Blue (c) Black (d) Pink

5. Four friends took part in a maths olympiad. Tipsy scored more than Mark, but less than Ginny. Ginny does not scored the highest marks. Rax scored more than Tipsy. Who among them scored the least?
(a) Ginny (b) Rax (c) Tipsy (d) Mark

Direction (Q. Nos. 6-7) *Observe the positions of teddies and answer the questions that follow.*

A B C D E F G H

6. If teddy E is removed from the sequence, then which teddy is third to the left of G?
(a) D (b) C (c) B (d) A

7. If one more teddy I is added after H in the sequence, then how many teddies are there after F?
(a) 5 (b) 2 (c) 4 (d) 3

8. Which number will come in place of question mark?

(a) 35 (b) 29 (c) 32 (d) 40

9. Count the number of rectangles in the figure shown below

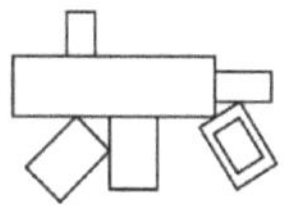

(a) 8 (b) 7
(c) 6 (d) 10

10. Find the mirror image of the figure shown below.

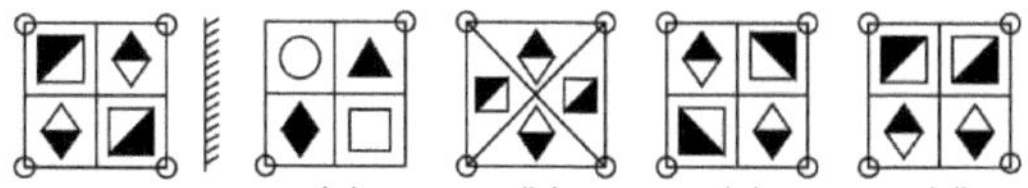

(a) (b) (c) (d)

11. Which number from the given options will replace the question mark?

21 – 64 – 43 18 – 48 – 30 32 – ? – 18

(a) 48 (b) 45 (c) 40 (d) 50

12. A pattern is drawn on a piece of paper. Which figure from the given alternatives will complete the given pattern?

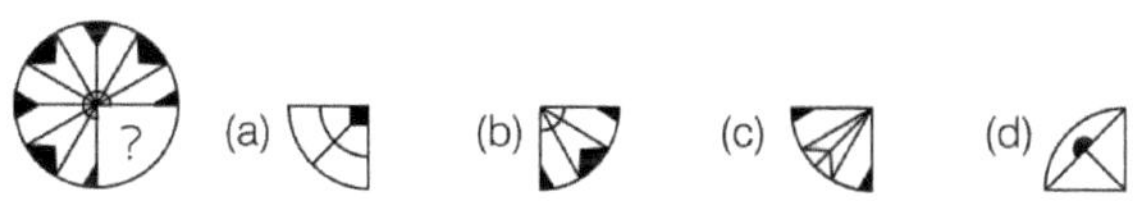

13. In which figure the given shape (X) is hidden?

(X) (a) (b) (c) (d)

14. Which word from the given alternatives cannot be formed using the letters of the given word?

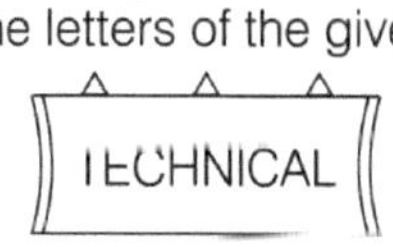

(a) NICE (b) CHIN (c) EACH (d) THREAD

15. In the shop of a fruits vendor. Fruits are kept as shown below

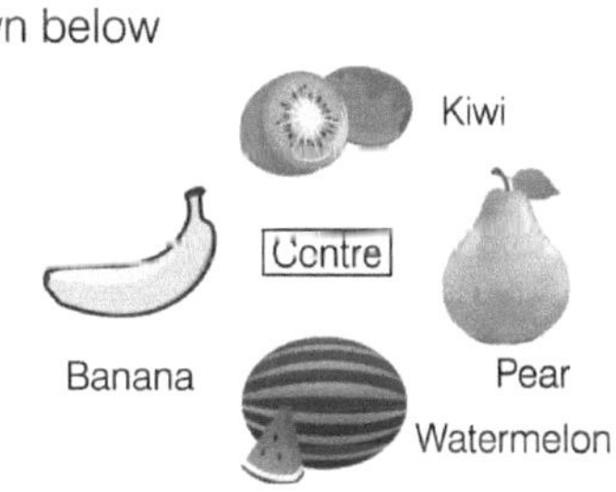

Which fruit is kept in the North direction?
(a) Banana (b) Kiwi (c) Pear (d) Pear

Practice Set 2

A Test Based on the Whole Content

1. TURN is to URN, as FLITE is to
(a) LITE (b) TILE (c) ELIT (d) FILT

2. Arrange the given letters to form a meaningful word and then find its number arrangement.

L	A	T	E	B
1	2	3	4	5

(a) 14325 (b) 21435 (c) 43251 (d) 32514

Direction (Q. Nos. 3) *Below are given some pictures. Observe their directions and answer the questions that follow.*

3. Cafe is in which direction in the above picture?
(a) North (b) East (c) South (d) West

4. What is the mirror image of the letters given below?

5. Some balls are shown following some pattern

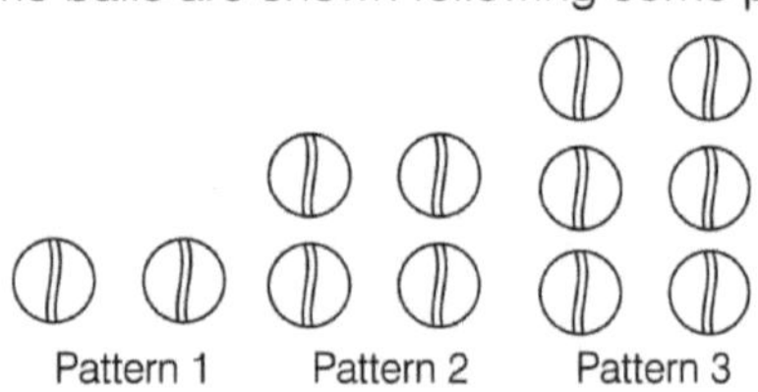

How many balls are there in the pattern 5?
(a) 10 (b) 8
(c) 7 (d) 12

6. In a certain code,  is called 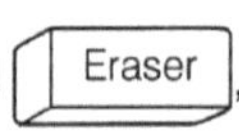, 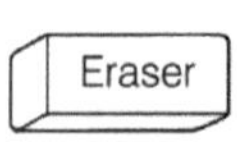 is called 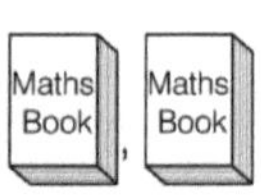 is called  and  is called , then what is used to write the text?

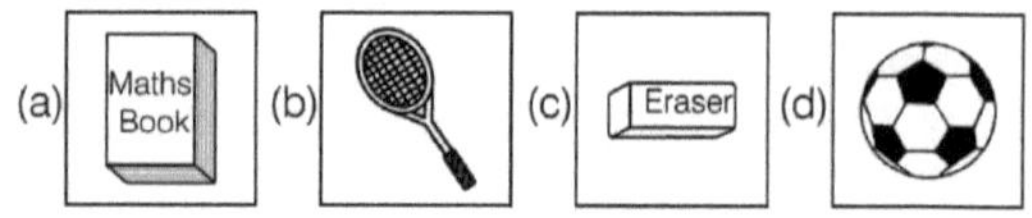

7. Which one is different?

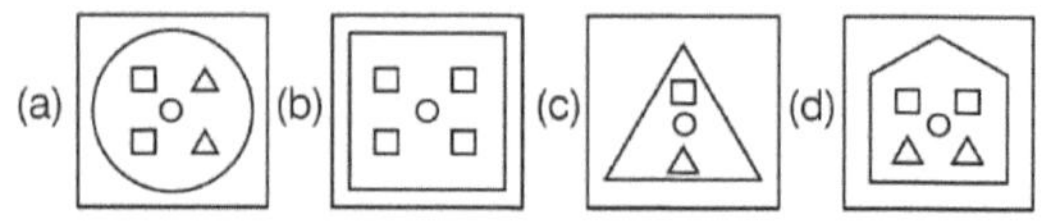

8. Count the number of circles in the figure shown below.

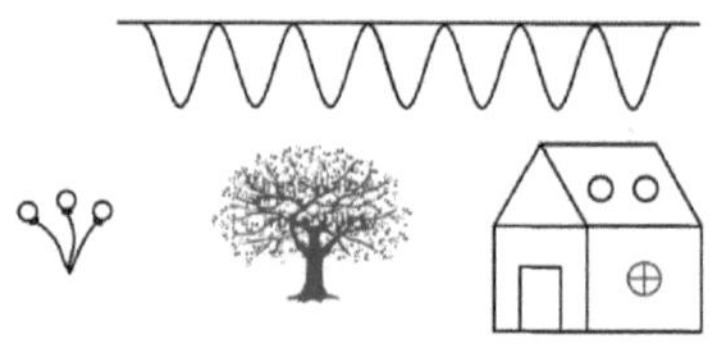

(a) 5
(b) 6
(c) 4
(d) 7

9. Which part from the given alternatives is hidden in the given figure(X)?

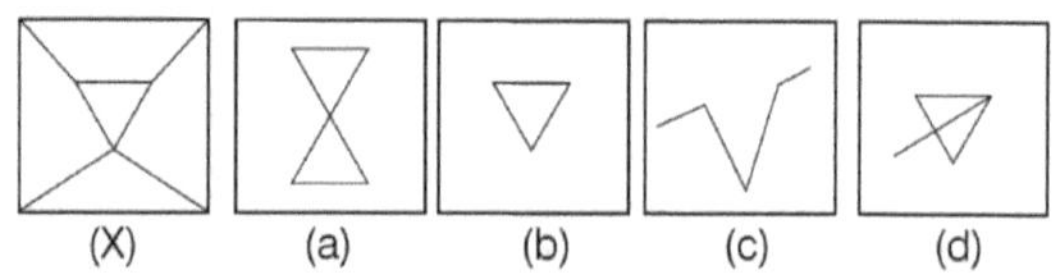

10. Which word from the given options can be formed using the letters of the word?

MATHEMATICS

(a) RATE (b) STICK (c) STATE (d) HEAR

11. Find the missing number.

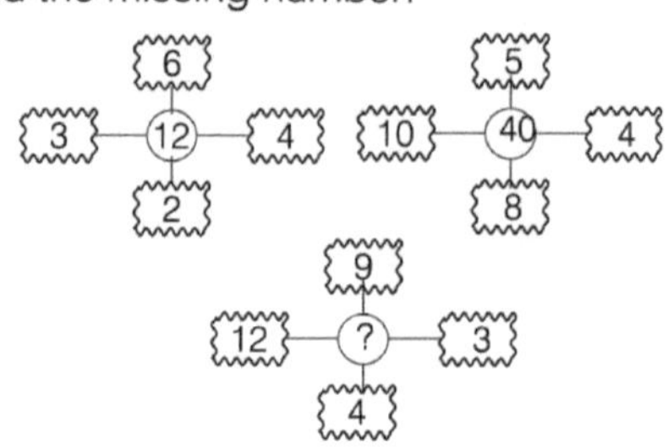

(a) 30 (b) 15 (c) 13 (d) 36

12. Complete the pattern given below by using the figures in the options.

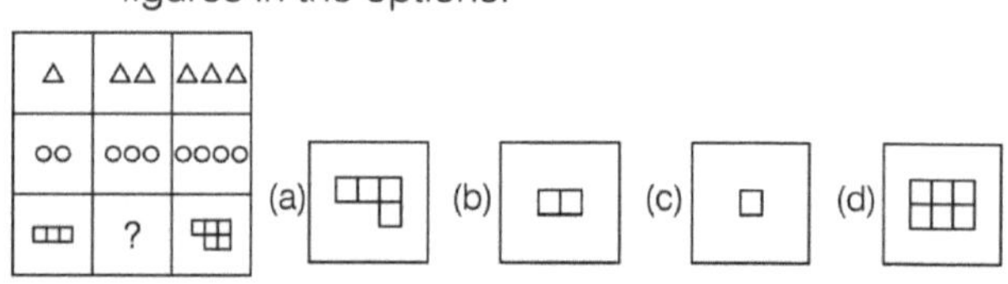

Answers and Explanations

1 Matching Pairs

1. (b) As, lock and key are used together. In the same way, needle and thread are used together.

2. (a) As, ice-cream cone is of cone shape. In the same way, cube face is of square shape.

3. (c) In the first pair of figures, two slanting lines are added in the middle of the first figure to get the second figure. Similarly, in the second pair, two slanting lines must be added in the middle part of the first figure to get the second figure.

So, figure in option (c) will complete the second pair.

4. (b) In the first pair of figures, first figure is divided into two and its right part is shown as the second figure with three circles in it. Similarly, the rectangle should be divided into two and its right part must be shown as the second figure with three circles in it.

So, figure in option (b) is the missing figure.

5. (c) In the first pair, first figure is pointing upwards and second figure is pointing downwards, but the lines are different at the end.

Similarly, in the second pair, the second figure must point downwards and the line at the end must be same as that of second figure in the first pair. So, figure in option (c) will complete the pattern.

6. (b) As, $4 \times 2 = 8$, similarly $7 \times 2 = \boxed{14}$

So, number in the fourth balloon should be '14'.

7. (b) As, $10 + 10 = 20$, similarly $50 + 10 = 60$

So, the price of fourth ice-cream is 60.

8. (d) As, P $\xrightarrow{\text{Next}}$ Q $\xrightarrow{\text{Next}}$ [R] Similarly, D $\xrightarrow{\text{Next}}$ E $\xrightarrow{\text{Next}}$ [F]

So, F is the missing letter.

9. (c) As, F $\xrightarrow{G}$ H, G $\xrightarrow{H}$ I Similarly, U $\xrightarrow{V}$ [W], V $\xrightarrow{W}$ [X]

So, the missing letters are 'WX'.

10. (d) The pattern is as follows

As, C ⟶ 3 (position of C in English alphabet)
+2 ↓
E ⟶ 5 (position of E in English alphabet)

Similarly, I ⟶ 9 (position of I in English alphabet)
+2 ↓
K ⟶ 11 (position of K in English alphabet)

So, K11 should come in place of question mark.

11. (a) As, T U V W X Y (+1 +1 +1 +1 +1)

Similarly, I J K [L M N] (+1 +1 +1 +1 +1)

So, the missing letters are 'LMN'.

12. (b) The first letter of the word TRAIN is removed to get the word RAIN. Similarly, the first letter of the word PAGE is to be removed to get the word AGE.

13. (b) As, onion is a vegetable, similarly cherry is a fruit.

14. (d) As, tongue is used to taste the food. Similarly, ears are used to hear the sound.

15. (a) As, bird flies in the sky. Similarly, duck swims in the water

2 Odd One Out

1. (b) Except dog all are birds.

2. (d) Except the clock in option (d), the hands in all the clocks are in straight line.

3. (c) In all the options except option (c), the sparrow is standing while in option (c) it is sitting down.

4. (c) Figure in option (c) i.e. circle is different from other figures, because they are made up of lines.

5. (d) In all the figures except option (d), both the shapes are on opposite sides to each other, whereas in option (d), the shapes are on the same side.

6. (c) All the figures except figure in option (c) are having same number of elements inside the main figure. So, figure (c) is different from others.

7. (c) Except letter 'E', all others are made up of three lines, whereas letter 'E' is made up of four lines.

8. (d) In the letters' group except in ontion (d) first and last letters are same. So, option (d) is odd one out.

9. (b) Except truck, all others are electronics items.

10. (d) The pattern in the letters' group is as follows

$F \xleftarrow[E]{} D,\ M \xleftarrow[L]{} K,\ V \xleftarrow[U]{} T$ But, $R \xleftarrow[Q,\,P]{} O$

So, 'RO' does not belong to the group.

11. (c) Except bat with number '5', all others are even number, whereas bat '5' is an odd number bat. So, it is different.

12. (c) Rain is the source of water and the water gets collected in Pond, River and Lake. So, Rain is different.

13. (b) Except '809' in all the numbers, '2' is at ten's place.

So, '809' does not belong to the group.

14. (c) Nail, needle and screw have one pointed side, whereas hammer is different, so it is different from others.

15. (b) In all the numbers except 26, '3' is added in the first digit to get the second digit, whereas in '26', '4' added in 2 to get 6.

3 What Comes Next?

1. (a) Elements in the first and third balloons are same. Elements in the second and fourth balloons are same. So, the next balloon will be same as first and third.

2. (c) First and fifth dolls are same. So, the sixth doll should be same as the second doll, as given in option (c).

3. (b) First and fifth figures are same. So, the second and sixth figures must be same. Therefore the next figure will be as shown in option (b).

4. (a) In pattern 1st, there are 3 teddies; in pattern 2nd, there are 6 teddies and in pattern 3rd, there are 9 teddies.

So, the pattern is as follows

$$3 \xrightarrow{+3} 6 \xrightarrow{+3} 9 \xrightarrow{+3} 12 \xrightarrow{+3} \boxed{15}$$

Thus, there should be 15 teddies in pattern 5th.

5. (a) In the first figure, upper left part and lower right part is shaded. In the second figure, upper right part and lower left part is shaded. As we see in the figures this pattern is repeated alternatively.

So, figure in option (a) should come in place of question mark(?).

6. (b) The water in the glass decreases gradually in every successive glass.

So, the next glass should be as shown in option (b).

7. (c) The squares in the circle increase by two in every next figure. So, there should be eight squares in the last figure as shown in figure in option (c).

8. (c) First and third figures are same only the elements in the rectangle reduce by one. Similarly, the second and fourth figures must be same with two triangles in rectangles in fourth figure.

9. (a) In every next figure, one circle at the end of each side is added and shaded square remains in the middle and alternatively circles are shaded.

So, figure in option (a) will be the next figure.

10. (b) The pattern is as follows

$$6 \xrightarrow{+6} 12 \xrightarrow{+6} 18 \xrightarrow{+6} \boxed{24}$$

So, '24' will continue the series.

11. (d) The pattern is as follows

Ist series, $2 \xrightarrow{+1} 3 \xrightarrow{+1} 4 \xrightarrow{+1} \boxed{5}$

IInd series, $4 \xrightarrow{+1} 5 \xrightarrow{+1} 6 \xrightarrow{+1} \boxed{7}$

So, '57' should come in place of question mark.

12. (a) The pattern is as follows

Ist series, $2 \xrightarrow{+1} 3 \xrightarrow{+1} 4 \xrightarrow{+1} \boxed{5}$

IInd series, $2 \xrightarrow{+1} 3 \xrightarrow{+1} 4 \xrightarrow{+1} \boxed{5}$

IIIrd series, $3 \xrightarrow{+1} 4 \xrightarrow{+1} 5 \xrightarrow{+1} \boxed{6}$

So, '556' is the missing number.

13. (a) The pattern is as follows

K → L → M → N → O → P → $\boxed{Q}$

So, 'Q' will be on the last paper a girl is holding.

14. The pattern is as follows
(d)
Ist series, M $\xrightarrow{+1}$ N $\xrightarrow{+1}$ O $\xrightarrow{+1}$ [P]

IInd series, D $\xrightarrow{+1}$ E $\xrightarrow{+1}$ F $\xrightarrow{+1}$ [G]

So, 'PG' will continue the series of letters.

15. The pattern is as follows
(a)
Ist series, P ‿Q‿ R ‿S‿ T ‿U‿ [V]

IInd series, Q ‿R‿ S ‿T‿ U ‿V‿ [W]

So, 'VW' will continue the series.

4 Let's Decode

1. The code of  is 'B' and the
(c) code of  is 'G'.

So, the code of   is 'BG'.

2. The code of  is 'T' and the
(a) code of  is 'F'.

So, the code of   is 'TF'.

3. The code of  is 'C' and the
(d) code of  is 'M'.

So, the code of   is 'CM'.

4. The code of  is 'M' and the
(c) code of  is 'G'.

So, the code of   is 'MG'.

5. The code of  is 'D' and the
(b) code of  is 'P'.

So, the code of   is 'DP'.

6. The codes of letters are as
(b) follow

P → e, A → 2, R → #, E → 4,
N → 1, T → $

So, the code of 'PARENT' is 'e2#41$'.

7. The codes of letters are as but
(d) follow

C → 0, O → ©, U → 8, N → 1,
T → $, R → #, Y → d

(a) So, the code of 'COUNTRY' is '0©81$#d'.

8. The colour of sky at night is
(a) Black, but here Black is called Green.

So, the colour of sky is Green at night.

9. The ring's shape is ○, but here ○
(c) is called □.

So, the geometrical shape □ is ring.

10. The national bird of India is
(d) 'Peacock', but here 'Peacock' is called 'Crow'. So, 'Crow' is the national bird of India.

11. 'Scooter' is a two wheeler
(c) vehicle, but here 'Scooter' is called Truck. So, 'Truck' is a two wheeler vehicle.

12. The second day after
(a) 'Saturday' is 'Monday', but here 'Monday' is called Tuesday.

So, the second day after 'Saturday' is 'Tuesday'.

13. 'Eraser' is used to erase the
(b) text, but here 'Eraser' is called 'Sharpener'.

So, 'Sharpener' is used to erase the text.

14. The capital of India is
(a) 'Delhi', but here 'Delhi' is called Mumbai.

So, 'Mumbai' is the capital of India.

5 Alphabet Test

1. 'E' will end the first word
(c) 'ONE' and start the second word 'EAT'.

2. 'L' will end the first word
(d) 'MALL' and start the second word 'LAKE'.

3. Letter 'I' when replaced with
(b) question mark will make the name of fruit KIWI and name of vegetable TURNIP.

4. Letter 'D' should be replaced
(d) with question mark to make the name of two amphibians CROCODILE and TADPOLE.

5. The word formed after
(a) arranging the given letters is ORANGE, which is a fruit.

6. The word formed after
(d) arranging the given letters is MARCH, which is a month.

7. The given letters when
(d) arranged form a meaningful word CLOCK and the correct combination of numbers is 31452.

8. The given letters when
(b) arranged will form a word GREAT and the correct combination of numbers is 24135.

9. (c) The word 'MIND' can be formed using the letters of the given word EXAMINED.

10. (d) The word 'GOAL' can be formed using the letters of the given word LOGICAL.

11. (c) The word 'GAME' cannot be formed using the letters of the given word LAUGHTER.

12. (b) 'TRUST' word cannot be formed using the letters of the given word TRANSPORT.

Solution (Q. Nos. 13-15)

13. (a) The given letter series is as follows.

A B C D E F G H I J K L M Z [Y] X W V U T S R Q P O N

(Left end) 15th from left (Right end)

So, it is clear from the above series that Y is fifteenth from the left end.

14. (d) The arrangement can be shown as

I J K L M Z Y X

6

So, it is clear that there are 6 letters between I and X.

15. (d) The given series after the removal of vowels can be shown as

B C D F G H J K L M Z Y X W V [T] S R Q P N

So, it is clear that 'T' is just after 'V' in the given series.

16. (a) The new letter sequence is ECNABRUTSID. Clearly, S comes after T.

17. (d) Meaningful words are ROSE, SORE and EROS. So, three words can be formed using the given letters.

6 Finding Positions

1. (b) The positions of the toys hanging in a toy shop can be shown as

A B C [D] E F G H I J K L

Left ← 5th to the left Right

So, D is fifth to the left of I.

2. (c) The arrangement of the books can be shown as

Top
K
L ↓ 3rd from the top
[M]
N ↑
O 5th from the bottom
P
Q
Bottom

So, M is at 5th position from the bottom.

Solution (Q. Nos. 3-4)

3. (b) Tree S is between tree R and tree T and this can be seen from the given arrangements as

R S [T]

4. (c) The arrangement can be shown as

P Q R S T [U] V

Left → 4th to the right Right

So, U is 4th to the right of tree Q.

5. (b) The positions of teddies after interchanging can be shown as.

D E J G [H] I F K

Left ← 2nd to the left Right

So, H is second to the left of F when F and J interchange their positions.

Solution (Q. Nos. 6-7)

6. (d) The arrangement/position of the boys can be shown as

Left ← 1 2 3 4 5 6 7 8 9 10 Right

③

So, there are 3 boys behind the boy at 4th position.

7. (c) After interchanging the positions the arrangement is as

Left 1 8 3 4 ⑤ 6 7 2 9 10 Right

→ 3rd to the right

So, boy at 5th position is third to the right of 8th boy after interchanging.

Solution (Q. Nos. 8-9)

8. (b) As, we see from the arrangement, teddy C is at 5th position from the right end.

9. (d) When teddy F is removed from the row, then teddy E is to the immediate left of teddy G, which can be shown as

Left A B C D [E] ~~F~~ G Right

← Immediate left

10. (c) The arrangement after the removal of flowers can be shown as.

③

Left 1 2 ~~3~~ 4 5 6 7 8 ~~9~~ 10 Right

So, there are three flowers between 5th and 10th flowers.

Solution (Q. Nos. 11-12)

11. (a) The arrangement of the ice-cream cones in the stand can be shown as

E F G H I J K L M N
← Left ⑤ Right

So, it is clear that there are 5 ice-cream cones to the left of cone J.

12. (d) The arrangement of the ice-cream cones after the removal of cones G and M can be shown as

E F ~~G~~ H [I] J K L ~~M~~

As, we see the arrangement, cone I is in the middle of the stand.

13. (c) The four persons according to their weights can be arranged as

Emme > Bryan > Ela > Tina

So, Emme is heaviest among all.

14. (d) The four friends according to their height can be arranged as

Mike Novak Rafael Maria

So, Maria is smallest among four friends.

15. (b) The arrangement of students according to the marks scored by them can be shown as

Harry > Peter > Bob > Andy

From the above arrangement, it is clear that Harry scored the highest marks.

[here, '>' symbol is used to show more than]

7 Directions

1. (a) The directions of the places can be shown as

House (North)

Grocery shop (West) (Centre) Church (East)

Temple (South)

So, it is clear that house is in the North direction from the Temple.

2. (c) The place which is in the West direction can be shown as

Grocery shop (West) ⟷ Church (East)

So, it is clear that grocery shop is in the West direction.

3. (b) The directions of the toys in which they are kept can be shown as

Kitty (North)

Cat (West) (Centre) Monkey (East)

Elephant (South)

So, it is clear from above that cat is in the West direction from the monkey.

4. (a) The toy which is in the North direction can be shown as

Kitty (North)
↕
Elephant (South)

So, from above it is clear that Kitty is in the North direction.

5. (d) The item which is in the West direction can be shown as

Cock (West) ⟷ Fruits basket (East)

So, it is clear that cock is in West direction.

6. (a) The directions of items can be shown as

Clock (North)

Cock (West) (Centre) Fruits basket (East)

Briefcase (South)

So, it is clear from above that clock is in the North direction.

Solution (Q. Nos. 7-8) The directions in the map of India can be shown as

7. (d) It is clear from the above map of India and the given options that Kerala is in the South direction.

8. (a) Gujarat is in the West direction from Jharkhand as shown in the above map.

9. (c) The direction in which Martin is standing can be shown as

Tom (North)
Harry (West) Centre Julia (East)
Martin (South)

So, it is clear from above that Martin is standing in South direction.

10. (b) The person standing in the East direction can be shown as

Harry (West) ⟷ Julia (East)

So, Julia is standing in the East direction.

8 Pattern Completion

1. (d) The given pattern can be completed by using the figure in option (d).

2. (c) The pattern can be completed by using the figure in option (c).

3. (c) The pattern can be completed by using the figure in option (c).

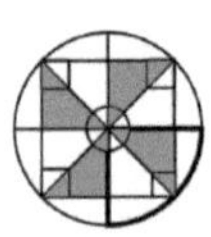

4. (d) The given pattern can be completed by using the figure in option (d).

5. (b) The pattern is as follows
As, $8+4+5+6=23$ and $5+3+9+15=32$
Similarly, $12+8+4+6=30$
So, 30' is the missing number.

6. (c) The pattern is as follows
$67-32=35, 82-45=37$ and $96-54=42$
So, '42' is the missing number.

7. (a) The pattern is as follows
$6\times5=30,\ 4\times7=28$ and $7\times9=63$
So, '63' is the missing number.

8. (b) The pattern is as follows
$9-6=3, 8-5=3$
$23-19=4, 15-11=4$
and $18-13=5, 36-31=5$
So, '5' will replace the question mark.

9. (d) Number outside the inner figure is the sum of the number inside the figure.
The patter is as follows.
$4+8=12,\ 8+7=15, 7+6=13$
and $4+6=10$
So, '10' is the missing number.

10. (a) The number inside the triangle is the multiplication of the numbers in the two circles.
The pattern can be shown as
$8\times3=24, 3\times2=6, 2\times5=10$
$5\times3=15, 7\times3=21$
and $7\times8=\boxed{56}$
So, '56' is the missing number.

11. (c) The pattern in the given figure is as follows
As, $23-18=5,\ 30-23=7$
and $47-30=17$
Similarly, $47-18=29$
So, '29' will replace the question mark.

12. (b) In each row, number of elements of the same type increases by 1.
So, figure in option (b) is the missing figure in the given pattern.

9 Mirror Images

1. (b) The mirror image of the picture is given in option (b) as shown below.

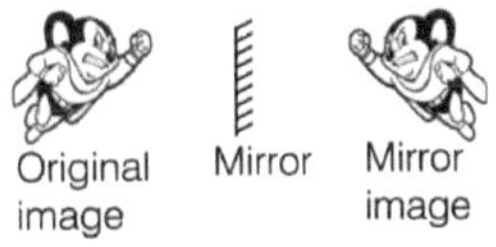

2. (b) The correct mirror image of the dog standing beside the mirror is given in option (b) as shown below.

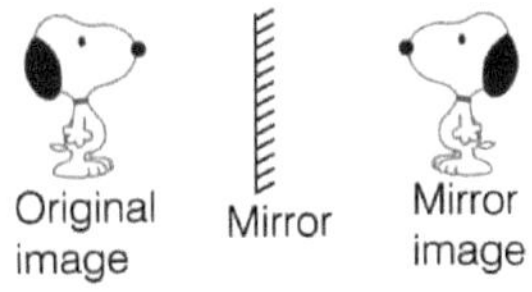

3. (d) The mirror image of the Jake's photograph is given in option (d) as shown below.

4. (b) The toy will appear in the mirror as given in option (b) as shown below.

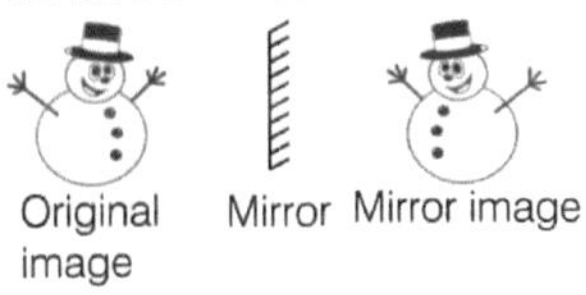

5. (d) The mirror image of kitty is given in option (d) as shown below.

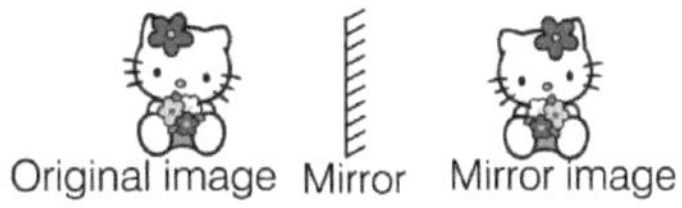

6. (d) The correct mirror image of the figure is given in option (d) as shown below.

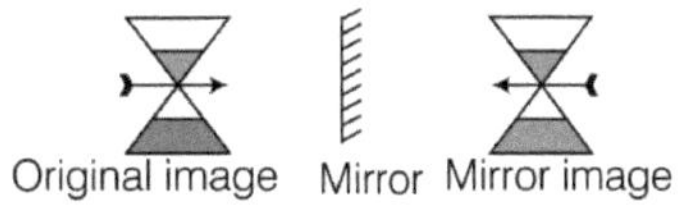

7. (d) The mirror image of the block is given in option (d) as shown below.

8. (b) The correct mirror image of the given pattern is given in option (b) as shown below.

9. (c) The correct mirror image of the block is given in option (c) as shown below.

10. (d) The mirror image of the numbers is given in option (d) as shown below.

11. (c) The correct mirror image of the numbers is given in option (c) as shown below.

12. (d) The letters written on the T-shirt, a man is wearing will appear in the mirror as given in option (d) which is as shown below.

13. (c) The mirror image of the word written outside the shop is given in option (c) as shown below.

14. (b) The mirror image of the code is given in option (b) as shown below.

10 Hidden Figures

1. (b) The given shape is hidden in the picture in option (b) as shown in adjacent figure.

2. (a) The given shape is hidden in the figure in option (a) as shown in adjacent figure.

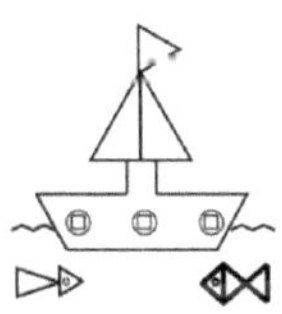

3. (b) The missing part shown in figure (X) belongs to the toy picture in option (b) as shown in adjacent figure.

4. (b) The given shape is hidden in the figure in option (b) as shown in adjacent figure.

5. (b) The given shape is hidden in the figure in option (b) as shown in adjacent figure.

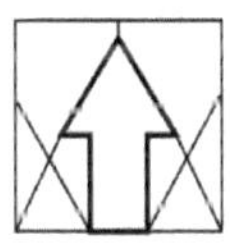

6. (c) The given shape is hidden in option figure (c) as its part as shown in adjacent figure.

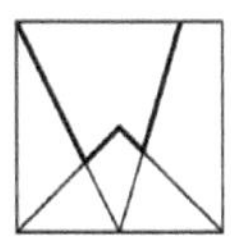

7. (d) The given shape is hidden in the figure in option (d) as shown in adjacent figure.

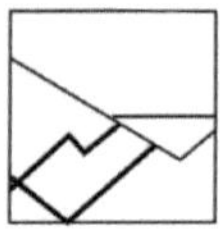

8. (b) The given part belongs to the figure in option (b) as shown in adjacent figure.

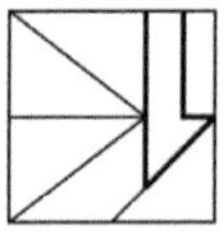

9. (d) Figure in option (d) is hidden in triangle shaped pattern as shown in adjacent figure.

10. (d) Figure in option (d) is exactly hidden in the given figure (X) as shown in adjacent figure.

11. (a) Figure in option (a) is hidden in the given figure (X) as shown in adjacent figure.

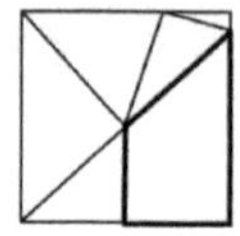

12. (c) Figure in option (c) is hidden in the given figure as shown in adjacent figure.

11 Geometrical Shapes

1. (c) The given picture can be labelled as shown below.

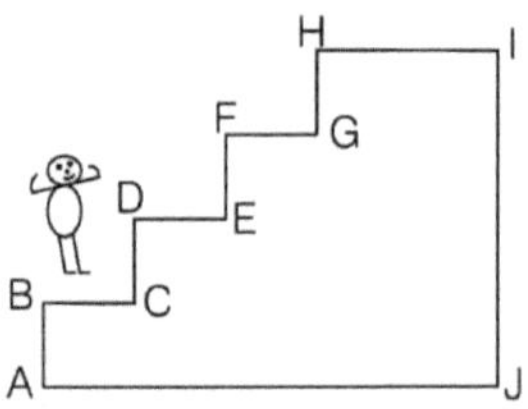

Number of straight lines = AB, BC, CD, DE, EF, FG, GH, HI, IJ, AJ = 10

2. (b) There are four different closed shapes in the given picture which are circle, triangle, square and rectangle.

3. (a) The number of slant lines in the given picture of X-mas tree can be shown as

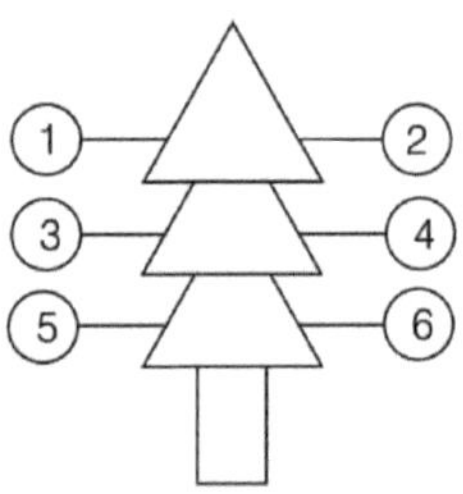

So, there are six slant lines as we count.

4. (c) In the given figure the triangles are shown as

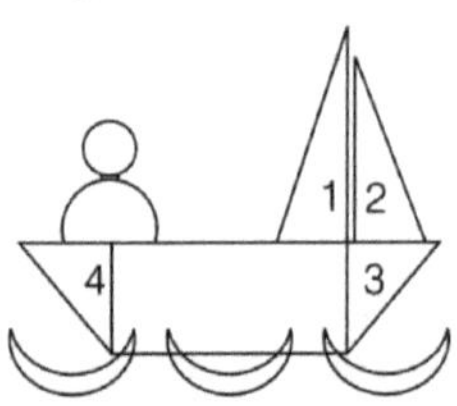

So, there are 4 triangles.

5. (d) In the given picture four different shapes are there which are circle, star, triangle and rectangle.

6. (c) The picture can be labelled as shown below

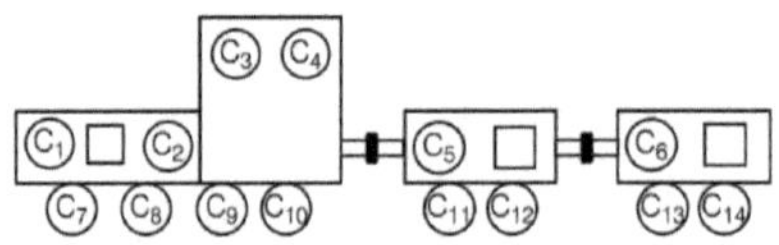

So, the number of circles in the above picture is 14.

7. (a) The picture can be labelled as shown below

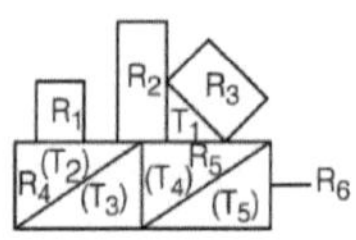

So, there are six rectangles and five triangles.

8. (c) From the given figures, only figure in option (c) i.e. cone is used to form the ice-cream cone.

9. (b) The given picture can be labelled as shown below

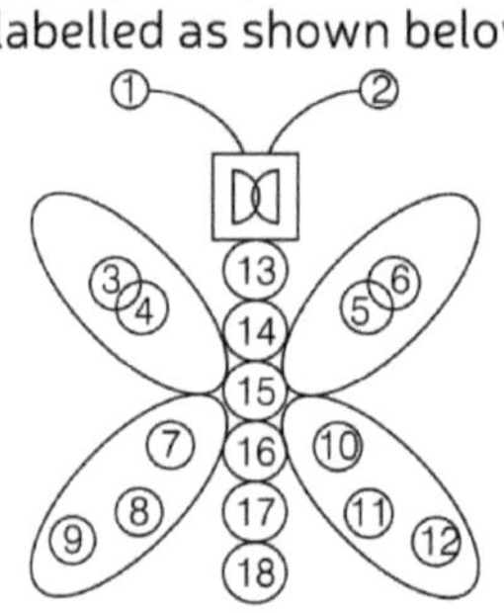

So, there are 18 circles in the given picture.

10. (a) The given shape of kite can be labelled as

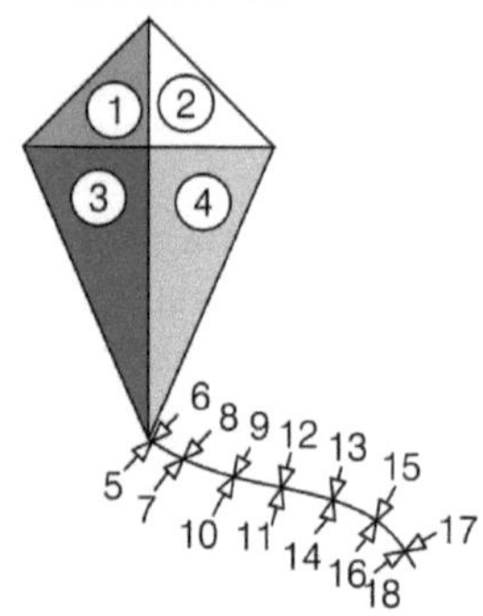

Number of triangles as they are labelled are 18 in numbers, but there are four more triangles which are formed by combining 1 & 2, 3 & 4, 1 & 3 and 2 & 4.

$\therefore$ Total number of triangles $= 18 + 4 = 22$

11. (c) The picture can be labelled as shown below

So, there are 8 rectangles in the given picture.

Solution (Q. Nos. 12-13) The given picture can be labelled as shown below

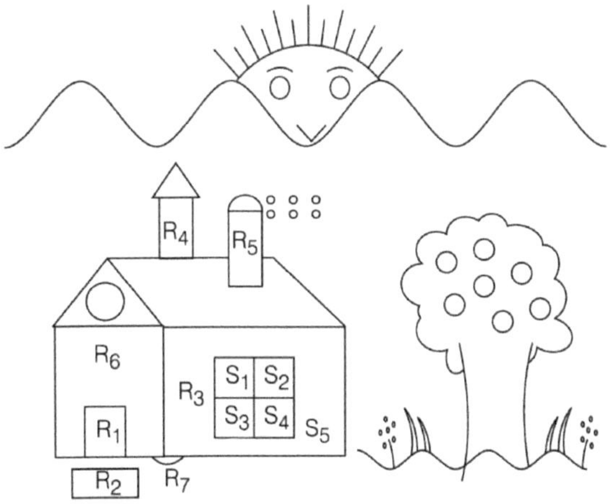

12. Number of rectangles is 7 in the above picture
(d) when they are counted.

Four more rectangles are formed by combining S_1 and S_2, S_3 and S_4, S_1 and S_3 and S_2 and S_4.

∴ Total number of rectangles $= 7 + 4 = 11$

13. Number of squares is 5 in the above picture as
(a) labelled in the picture.

Solution (Q. Nos. 14-15) The given picture can be labelled as shown below.

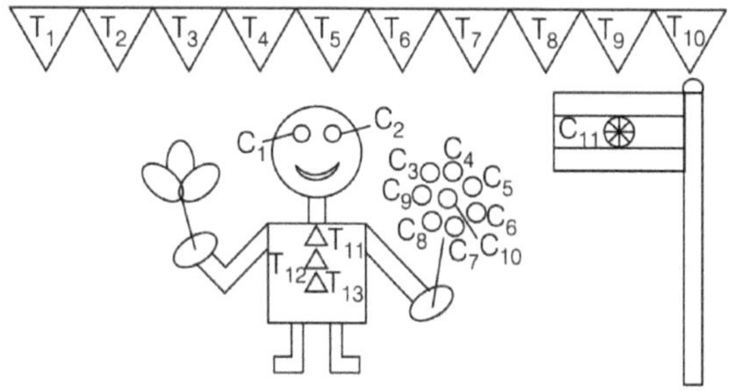

14. Number of triangles in the given picture is 13
(b) when they are counted.

15. ∵ Number of triangles = 13
(a) and number of circles = 11

∴ Required difference $= 13 - 11 = 2$

Practice Set 1

1. Except today, all others are
(d) week days. So, today does not belong to the group.

2. In first figure, one side is
(c) added to get the second figure. Similarly, one side must be added in the third figure to get the fourth figure which is given in option (c).

3. 'E' will end the first word
(c) PAGE and start the second word EACH.

4. The colour of Sunflower is
(a) yellow, but here yellow is called red.

So, the colour of Sunflower is red.

5. The four friends according to
(d) their marks can be arranged as

Rax > Ginny > Tipsy > Mark

So, it is clear that Mark scored the least.

6. The sequence of teddies
(b) after removing teddy E can be shown as follows

Left A B [C] D ~~E~~ F G H Right
← 3rd to the left

So, 'C' is third to the left of G.

7. The sequence of teddies can
(d) be shown as follows

Left A B C D E F G H I Right
→ ③

So, it can be seen that there are 3 teddies after F.

8. The pattern is as follows
(a)

$14 + 7 = 21$,

$21 + 7 = 28$,

$28 + 7 = \boxed{35}$

So, '35' will replace the question mark

9. The figure can be labelled as
(b) shown below.

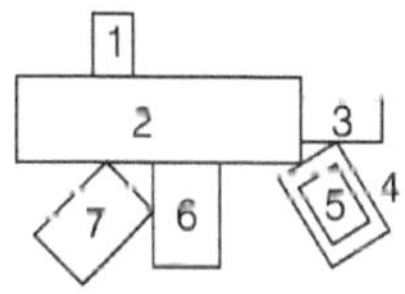

So, there are 7 rectangles as we count.

10. The mirror image of the
(c) given figure is shown in option (c).

11. (d) The pattern is as follows
As, $21+43=64$
(Number in middle)
$18+30=48$
(Number in middle)
Similarly, $32+18=\boxed{50}$
So, '50' will replace the question mark.

12. (b) The pattern can be completed by using the figure in option (b).

13. (a) The given shape (X) is hidden in option figure (a) as shown below

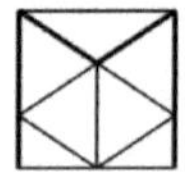

14. (d) The word THREAD cannot be formed using the letters of the given word TECHNICAL.

15. (b) The directions of the fruits can be shown as

Kiwi (North)
Banana (West) — Centre — Pear (East)
Watermelon (South)

So, it is clear that kiwi is kept in North direction.

Practice Set 2

1. (a) As the first letter of the word TURN is removed to get the word URN. Similarly, 'F' is removed to get the word 'LITE'

2. (d) The given letters can be arranged to form a meaningful word TABLE and the sequence is '32514'.

Solution (Q. Nos. 3)

The directions can be shown as

Car (North)
School (West) — Centre — Cafe (East)
Guava tree (South)

3. (b) Cafe is in East direction in the given arrangement of pictures.

4. (a) The letters given in option (a) is the correct mirror image of letters as shown below.

5. (a) The pattern is as follows
$2 \xrightarrow{+2} 4 \xrightarrow{+2} 6 \xrightarrow{+2} 8 \xrightarrow{+2} \boxed{10}$
So, '10' balls will be three in pattern 5.

6. (c)  is used to write the text, but here  is called [Eraser]. So, [Eraser] is used to write the text.

7. (c) In each figure, there are five elements, but the figure in option (c) consists of three element, so it is different.

8. (b) There are six circles in the given figure.

9. (b) The figure in option (b) is exactly hidden in the given figure and this can be shown as

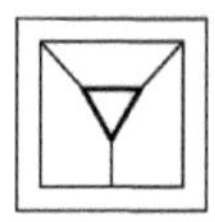

10. (c) The word STATE can be formed using the letters of the word MATHEMATICS.

11. (d) The pattern is as follow
As, $6\times2=12, 3\times4=12$ and $10\times4=40, 5\times8=40$
similarly, $9\times4=36, 12\times3=36$
So, '36' is the missing number.

12. (a) The figure in option (a) will complete the given pattern as number of elements increases by 1 in each block as we go from 1 to 2 and 2 to 3.

9 789352 512126